Welcome to
Microsoft®
Office 2013

JILL MURPHY
Custom Performance Solutions

ALEC FEHL
Asheville-Buncombe Technical Community College

CHRISTIE JAHN HOVEY
Lincoln Land Community College

LABYRINTH
LEARNING™

Berkeley, CA

Product Manager:
Brian Favro

Development Manager:
Laura Popelka

Production Manager:
Rad Proctor

eLearning Production Manager:
Arl S. Nadel

Indexing:
Joanne Sprott

Cover Concept:
Huckdesign

LABYRINTH
LEARNING™

Welcome to Microsoft Office 2013
by Jill Murphy, Alec Fehl, and Christie Jahn Hovey

Copyright © 2014 by Labyrinth Learning

Labyrinth Learning
2560 9th Street, Suite 320
Berkeley, California 94710
800.522.9746
On the web at lablearning.com

ITEM: 1-59136-659-3
ISBN-13: 978-1-59136-659-1

Manufactured in the United States of America.

0 9 8 7 6 5 4 3 2 1

Welcome to Microsoft Office 2013

Table of Contents

Quick Reference Table Summary

Preface

Welcome to Microsoft® Office 2013 provides a survey of Office 2013 applications. Students get an introduction to Word, Excel, PowerPoint, and Access. The book begins with four Word lessons, which cover topics such as the Ribbon, navigation techniques, AutoComplete, tables, editing text, AutoCorrect, character formatting, special text effects, and more. In the two Excel lessons, students enter and edit data, construct simple formulas, and depict data using column and pie charts. PowerPoint topics include creating a new presentation, working with layouts and design themes, creating animations and transitions, and more. And finally, in the Access lesson, students will create a new database and print datasheets.

Labyrinth Learning publishes easy-to-use textbooks that empower educators to teach complex subjects quickly and effectively, while enabling students to gain confidence, develop practical skills, and compete in a demanding job market. We add comprehensive support materials, assessment and learning management tools, and eLearning components to create true learning solutions for a wide variety of instructor-led, self-paced, and online courses.

Our textbooks follow the *Labyrinth Instructional Design,* our unique and proven approach that makes learning easy and effective for every learner. Our books begin with fundamental concepts and build through a systematic progression of exercises. Quick Reference Tables, precise callouts on screen captures, carefully selected illustrations, and minimal distractions combine to create a learning solution that is highly efficient and effective for both students and instructors.

This course is supported with *comprehensive instructor support* materials that include printable solution guides for side-by-side comparisons, test banks, customizable assessments, customizable PowerPoint presentations, detailed lesson plans, preformatted files for integration to leading learning management systems, and more. Our unique WebSims allow students to perform realistic exercises for tasks that cannot be performed in the computer lab.

Acknowledgements

We are grateful to the instructors who have used Labyrinth titles and suggested improvements to use over the many years we have been writing and publishing books. This book has benefited greatly from the reviews and suggestions of the following instructors.

Debra Blencowe, *Collin College*

Sara Bozzuto, *Middlesex Community College*

Gert Brailsford, *Global Business Institute*

Menka Brown, *Piedmont Technical College*

Brenda Gayle Bryant, *The Gayle Group*

John Bullock, *Kirkwood Community College*

Marie Calarco, *Cuyahoga Valley Career Center*

Beverly Campbell, *TCCD*

Sherryl Carter, *Inglewood Unified School District/Inglewood Community Adult School*

Robert Cook, *Martinez Adult Education*

Barbara R. Corzonkoff, *SMCOE/ROP and Skyline College*

Teresa Ferguson, *Seattle Vocational Institute*

Jason Holcomb, *Vatterott Educational Centers*

Gaylene Jones, *Summit College*

Kimberly Jones, *Bonds Career Center*

Dawn Kaiser, *Kirtland CC*

Kevin Keehan, *Southwestern College*

Vicky Kelder, *Westchester Community College*

Peggy Kozy, *University of Phoenix*

Joanne Lauzon, *North Shore Community College*

Elaine Loughrey, *MiraCosta College*

Samantha Marchant, *North GA Tech*

Nikkea Masters, *Placer School for Adults*

Tom McGinn, *YCCC*

Julie Meyer, *McKendree University*

Jerry Mitchell, *Institute of Business & Medical Careers*

Chidmma Nwankwere, *Hi-Tech Charities*

Chesty Peterson, *Downy Adult School*

Richard Peterson, *South Seattle Community College*

George Riley, *Pickaway-Ross JVS*

Joseph Roy, *Madison Area Technical College*

Joyce Schlose, *Goodwill Industries of Denver*

Doris Scott, *Traviss Career Center*

Greg Simos, *Jefferson College*

Lisa Smith, *Moore Norman Technology Center*

Mary Spata, *Wilco Career Center*

Judy Spencer, *Central Oklahoma Juvenile Center*

Michelle Story, *Illinois Valley Community College*

Visual Conventions

`Type this text`   Anything you should type at the keyboard is printed in this typeface.

 TIP!   Tips, Notes, and Warnings are used throughout the text to draw attention to certain topics.

Command→ Command   This convention indicates multiple selections to be made from a menu bar. For example, File→ Save means to select File and then to select Save

Command→ Command→ Command, etc.   This convention indicates how to give a command from the Ribbon. The commands are written: Ribbon Tab→Command Group→ Command→Subcommand.

FROM THE KEYBOARD   These notes indicate shortcut keys for executing a task described in the text.

QUICK REFERENCE   Quick Reference tables provide generic instructions for key tasks. Only perform these tasks if you are instructed to in an exercise.

     This icon indicates the availability of a web-based simulation for an exercise or some other online content. You may need to use a WebSim if your computer lab is not set up to support particular exercises.

     Hands-On exercises are introduced immediately after concept discussions. They provide detailed, step-by-step tutorials so you can master the skills presented.

     The Concepts Review section includes both true/false and multiple choice questions designed to gauge your understanding of the concepts introduced in the lesson.

     Skill Builder exercises provide additional hands-on practice with moderate assistance.

     Try This at Home exercises test your skills by describing the correct results without providing specific instructions on how to achieve them.

Word – Working with Word Basics

In this lesson, you will learn the basics of Microsoft Office Word 2013. You will start Word, work with the Ribbon interface, open a document, learn navigation techniques for moving around the document, and start a new document. Finally, you will get familiar with Word's Help feature.

LESSON OBJECTIVES

After studying this lesson, you will be able to:

- Identify key parts of the Word 2013 interface
- Open and close existing documents
- Start new documents
- Navigate in a document using scroll bars and the keyboard
- Use Word's Help feature
- Exit Word

Case Study: Exploring Word

Jasmine Morales will attend Central Community College in the fall, and she wants to learn Word 2013 to help with her school assignments. She just got a new laptop with Word 2013, and she's ready to explore the Word window.

She finds that Word's Ribbon interface is intuitive and easy to use.

Jasmine decides to practice using Word 2013 by manipulating a product brochure she received as an email attachment from a gardening store. The brochure is written in Word 2003. The Compatibility Mode indicator in the title bar lets Jasmine know the document was created in an earlier version of Word. She has the option of leaving the brochure in the Word 2003 format or converting it to the Word 2013 format.

If Jasmine wants to share the document with her gardening friend who uses Word 2003, she won't convert the document. If she wants to be able to use a document created in Word 2003 and also use all of Word 2013's new features, she will convert the document.

Discovering Just How Suite It Is

Microsoft Office 2013 is a suite of software programs. A suite is several programs usually sold together as one package, which is less expensive than buying them individually. In this course, you will learn to work with Word, Excel, PowerPoint, and Access—four of the most popular software programs in the Office 2013 suite.

- **Word 2013:** This word-processing program allows you to create documents, such as letters and envelopes, and then make changes without having to retype all of the information. Other examples of Word documents include memos, reports, and fancy flyers.

- **Excel 2013:** A spreadsheet program makes organizing numbers and financial information and performing calculations a breeze. A budget is a good example of something you might create in a spreadsheet program. Other ideas include sales reports, billing statements, and graphs.

- **PowerPoint 2013:** Whether you are giving a presentation to your community center or your work colleagues, PowerPoint lets you produce elegant electronic slide shows with little effort. The tools built into this program help make any presentation a hit!

- **Access 2013:** Organizing very large amounts of data is how a database program shines. If you have a collection of hundreds of CDs or an extensive parts inventory, you can keep track of them in a database.

One of the great things about a software suite is that all programs share common features and a similar design. This means that when you have learned one program, you can easily learn another. And, moving information between various programs in the suite is a snap.

Defining Word

Word 2013 is the name of the word-processing program that is part of the Microsoft Office 2013 suite of programs. As in all word-processing programs, you use Word 2013 to electronically create and edit text. After creating a document, you can make editing changes. You can make big changes, too, such as adding or deleting a couple of paragraphs in the middle of a page. When you do, the existing text moves out of the way to make room for the new text, or it collapses to close the gap when you delete text. Other editing changes, such as moving or copying text within a page or from one page to another, are also easy.

Word is great for formatting text, too. It also provides special features such as the Spelling & Grammar Checker. There's even an AutoCorrect feature that can fix many mistakes for you.

Starting Word 2013

The method you use to start Word and other Office 2013 programs depends on whether you are using the Windows 7 or Windows 8 operating system.

- **Windows 7:** Click Start , choose Microsoft Office from the All Programs menu, and then choose Word 2013.
- **Windows 8:** Locate the Word 2013 tile on the Windows Start screen; click the tile to start Word.

Viewing the Word Start Screen

The Word Start screen is the first screen you see when you start the program. It offers several ways to begin working. Don't be concerned if your Start screen is arranged differently from this example. You can rearrange the templates on the right side of the screen, and the appearance also depends on your screen's resolution.

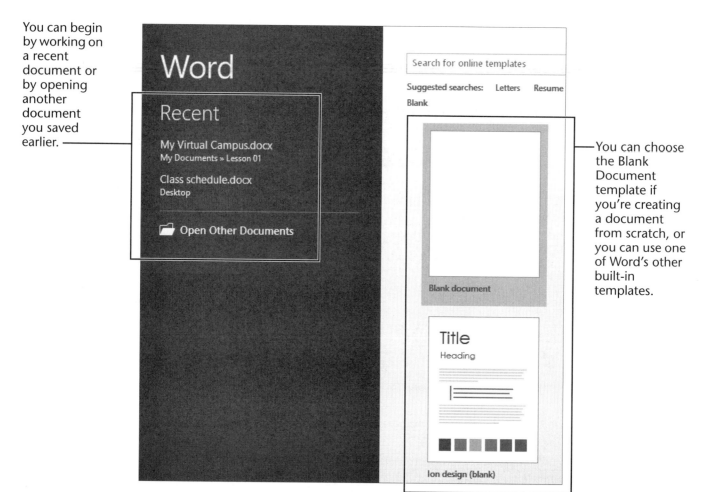

You can begin by working on a recent document or by opening another document you saved earlier.

You can choose the Blank Document template if you're creating a document from scratch, or you can use one of Word's other built-in templates.

HANDS-ON 1.1A **Start Word (Windows 8)**

Windows 7 Users: Skip this exercise.

In this exercise, you will start the Word program.

1. If necessary, start your computer.
   The Windows Start screen appears.

2. Locate the **Word 2013** tile.

3. Click the tile to start Word.
   The Word program loads, and the Word Start screen appears.

4. Make sure the Word window is **maximized** ▭.

5. Click the **Blank Document** template to open the Word window.

 HANDS-ON 1.1B **Start Word (Windows 7)**

Windows 8 Users: Skip this exercise.

In this exercise, you will start the Word program.

1. If necessary, start your computer.
   The Windows Desktop appears.

2. Click **Start** ⊞ at the left edge of the taskbar and choose **All Programs**.

3. Choose **Microsoft Office**, and then choose **Microsoft Word 2013** from the menu.
   The Word program loads, and the Word Start screen appears.

4. Make sure the Word window is **maximized** ▭.

5. Click the **Blank Document** template to open the Word window.

Exploring the Word 2013 Window

The following illustration describes the main elements of the Word window. Don't be concerned if your document window looks somewhat different from this illustration. The Word screen is customizable.

The File tab leads to Backstage view, where you open, print, save, and close documents.

Frequently-used commands appear on the Quick Access toolbar.

Your document name and the application name appear in the title bar.

The Ribbon holds commands to create and edit your documents.

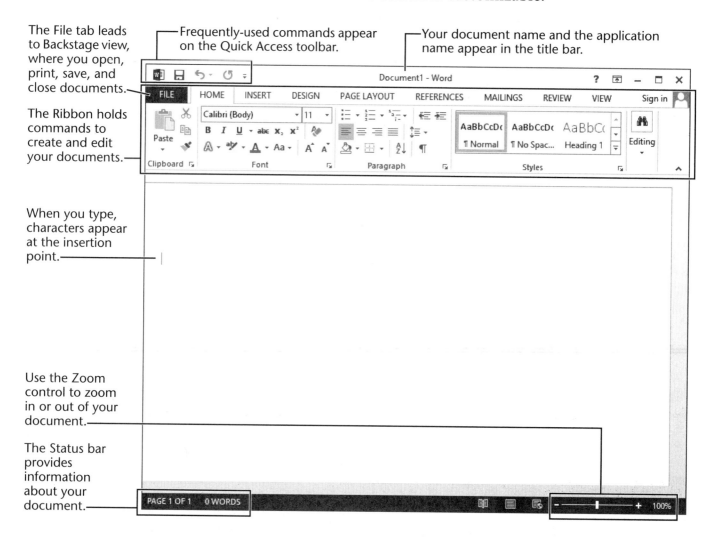

When you type, characters appear at the insertion point.

Use the Zoom control to zoom in or out of your document.

The Status bar provides information about your document.

Introducing the Ribbon

The band running across the top of the screen is the Ribbon. This is where you find the commands you need to create, format, and edit your documents.

The Ribbon consists of three main elements:

- Tabs
- Groups
- Commands

The tabs include Home, Insert, Design, Page Layout, and so on. A group contains related commands within a tab. Groups on the Home tab, for example, include Clipboard, Font, Paragraph, Styles, and Editing. An example of a command in the Font group is the Bold command.

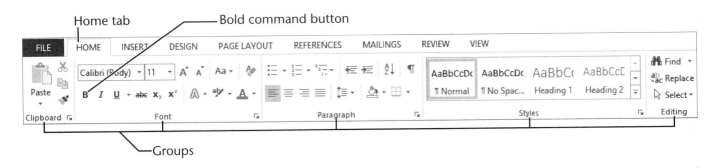

ToolTips

When you hover the mouse pointer over commands on the Ribbon, ToolTips may appear. These are little notes that contain command descriptions, and they often contain keystrokes that you can use instead of clicking commands with the mouse. In this example, you see the ToolTip for the Bold command. You can use [Ctrl]+[B] to execute the command rather than clicking the Bold button if you wish.

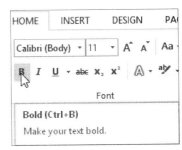

Contextual Tabs

Contextual tabs appear in context with the task you are performing. For example, if you are working with tables, the Table Tools tabs, Design and Layout, appear, as shown in the following illustration on the left. If you are working with clip art, the Picture Tools' Format tab appears, as shown in the following illustration on the right. You'll learn more about these tabs later in this course.

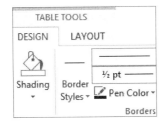

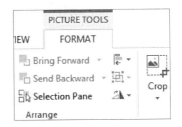

Varying Button Arrangements

The arrangement of buttons on the Ribbon can vary depending on your screen resolution and how the Word window is sized. Following are two examples of how the Paragraph group might appear on the Ribbon.

 TIP! It's usually a good idea to maximize 🗖 the program window so the buttons always appear the same.

Introducing the Toolbars

There are two important toolbars in Word 2013: the Quick Access toolbar and the Mini toolbar. You will work with these toolbars later in this course.

Quick Access Toolbar

The Quick Access toolbar in the upper-left corner of the screen contains frequently used commands. It operates independently from the Ribbon. Like the Ribbon, when you hover the mouse pointer over a button, Word displays a ToolTip describing the button and offers keystroke combinations you can use instead of clicking the button.

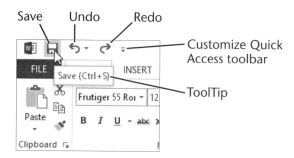

Mini Toolbar

The Mini toolbar contains frequently used formatting commands such as Bold and Italic. When you select (highlight) text, the Mini toolbar fades in so you can easily format the selected text.

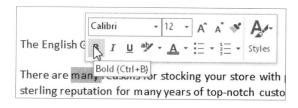

HANDS-ON 1.2 **Explore Ribbon Tabs and Groups**

In this exercise, you will explore various tabs and groups on the Ribbon.

1. Click the **Insert** tab on the Ribbon to display the commands available in that category.

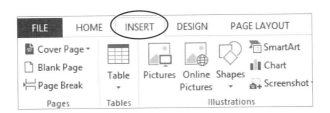

Notice the Pages, Tables, and Illustrations groups on the Insert tab.

2. Click the **Page Layout** tab.

This tab displays commands for arranging text on the page.

3. Feel free to examine more tabs on the Ribbon.

4. Click the **Home** tab.

Opening Documents

The Open command on the File tab displays the Open screen in Backstage view. Choose the basic location from the center panel. For example, if you want to open a document from your local computer, choose the Computer icon. This displays the open dialog box, and you can navigate to your file storage location from there.

The Open command in Backstage view.

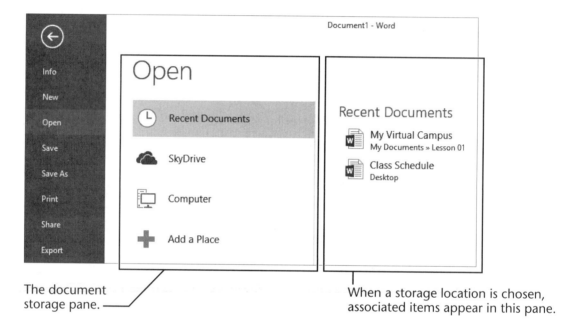

The document storage pane.

When a storage location is chosen, associated items appear in this pane.

Opening Older Word Documents

If you open a document created in a previous version of Word, it opens in Compatibility Mode. The term appears in the title bar, as shown in the following illustration. Older Word documents do not understand the new features in Word 2013, so those features are limited or disabled.

TIP! When an older document is open, a *Convert* command is available in Backstage view. Use it to upgrade the file and enable the new features of Office 2013 applications. The convert process overwrites the original file.

 HANDS-ON 1.3 **Open a Document**

In this exercise, you will open an existing document through the Open dialog box.

Before You Begin: Navigate to the student resource center to download the student exercise files for this book.

1. Click the **File** tab at the left end of the Ribbon, and then click the **Open** command from the panel on the left.

2. On the Open screen, choose your file storage location, such as Computer, from the center panel.

   You may need to consult with your instructor to determine how to navigate to your file storage location.

3. Follow these steps to open the English Gardener document:

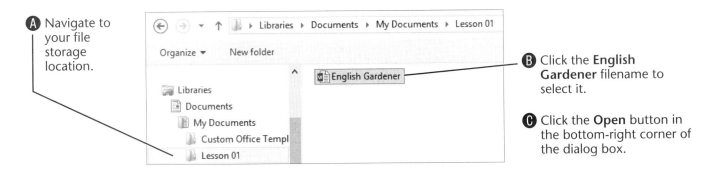

A Navigate to your file storage location.

B Click the **English Gardener** filename to select it.

C Click the **Open** button in the bottom-right corner of the dialog box.

Navigating in a Word Document

If you are working in a multipage document, it's helpful to know about various techniques for moving through documents. You can navigate using the scroll bar located at the right side of the screen, or you can use keystrokes.

Navigating with the Scroll Bar

The scroll bar lets you browse through documents; however, scrolling does not move the insertion point. After scrolling, you must click in the document where you want to reposition the insertion point.

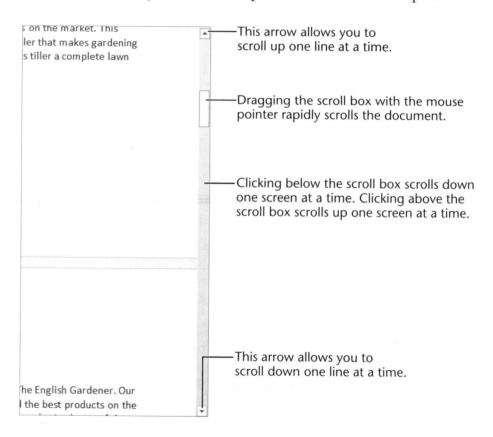

on the market. This
ler that makes gardening
s tiller a complete lawn

— This arrow allows you to scroll up one line at a time.

— Dragging the scroll box with the mouse pointer rapidly scrolls the document.

— Clicking below the scroll box scrolls down one screen at a time. Clicking above the scroll box scrolls up one screen at a time.

— This arrow allows you to scroll down one line at a time.

he English Gardener. Our
l the best products on the

Different Mouse Pointer Shapes

The mouse pointer must be shaped like an I-beam I when you want to position the flashing insertion point using the mouse. (You click the left mouse button to place the insertion point at the position of the I-beam.) The mouse pointer appears as an I-beam when between the document margins.

The mouse pointer appears as a white, right-tilting arrow when in the selection bar, which is located in the document's left margin. The white arrow is used to select (highlight) text. You will learn more about selecting text later in this course.

HANDS-ON 1.4 Scroll and Position the Insertion Point

In this exercise, you will use the scroll bar to move through a document. Then you will reposition the insertion point in the document.

1. Follow these steps to scroll in the document:

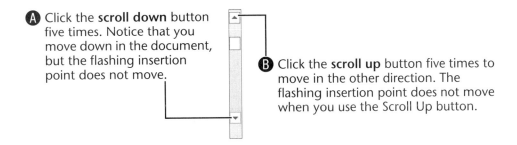

Ⓐ Click the **scroll down** button five times. Notice that you move down in the document, but the flashing insertion point does not move.

Ⓑ Click the **scroll up** button five times to move in the other direction. The flashing insertion point does not move when you use the Scroll Up button.

2. Slide the **I-beam** Ⅰ mouse pointer in the body of the document.

The mouse pointer looks like an I-beam when it's between the document margins.

3. Click the **I-beam** Ⅰ mouse pointer anywhere in the document to position the flashing insertion point.

If the background is highlighted, you accidentally dragged the mouse pointer and selected the text. Deselect by clicking the mouse pointer in the document background, and try again.

4. Move the mouse pointer into the left margin area.

The white arrow shape is now visible.

5. In the first paragraph, position the **I-beam** Ⅰ mouse pointer in the first line and click.

The insertion point appears just where you clicked.

6. Click the open part of the **scroll bar** below the scroll box to move down one screen.

7. Drag the **scroll box** down with the mouse pointer until the end of the document is visible.

8. Click the **I-beam** I mouse pointer at the end of the text to position the insertion point on the last page.

9. Drag the **scroll box** to the top of the scroll bar; then, click the **I-beam** I mouse pointer in front of the first word of the first paragraph.

Navigating with the Keyboard

Whether you use the mouse or the keyboard to navigate through a document is a matter of personal preference. Navigating with the keyboard always moves the insertion point so it will be with you when you arrive at your destination. The following table provides keystrokes for moving quickly through a document.

KEYBOARD NAVIGATION TECHNIQUES

Press	To Move
→	One character to the right
←	One character to the left
Ctrl + →	One word to the right
Ctrl + ←	One word to the left
↓	Down one line
↑	Up one line
PageDown	Down one screen
PageUp	Up one screen
Ctrl + End	To the end of the document
Ctrl + Home	To the beginning of the document
End	To the end of the line
Home	To the beginning of the line

 HANDS-ON 1.5 **Use the Keyboard to Navigate**

In this exercise, you will use the keyboard to move through a document.

1. Click the **I-beam** I mouse pointer in the middle of the first line of the second paragraph.

2. Tap the right arrow → and left arrow ← keys a few times to move to the right and left one character at a time.

3. Tap the up arrow ↑ and the down arrow ↓ keys a few times to move up and down, one line at a time.

4. Hold down Ctrl and keep it down, and then tap Home to move to the beginning of the document. Release Ctrl.

5. Use the arrow keys to position the insertion point in the middle of the first line of the first paragraph.

6. Hold down Ctrl and keep it down, and then tap the left arrow ← key a few times to move to the left, one word at a time. Release Ctrl.

7. Hold down Ctrl and keep it down, and then tap the right arrow → key several times to move to the right, one word at a time. Release Ctrl.

8. Tap Home to move to the beginning of the line.

9. Tap End to move to the end of the line.

10. Tap PageDown and PageUp to scroll down and up one screen at a time.

Closing Documents

You close a file by clicking File tab and choosing the Close command from the panel on the left in Backstage view.

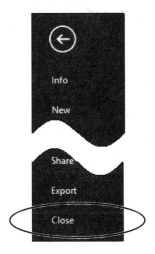

If you haven't saved your document, Word will prompt you to save it.

HANDS-ON 1.6 **Close the Document**

In this exercise, you will close your file.

1. Click the **File** tab and choose **Close** from the panel on the left.

2. Click **Don't Save** if Word asks if you want to save changes.

3. If a blank document is on the screen, use the same technique to close it.

   The document window below the Ribbon is completely blank when all documents are closed.

Starting a New Blank Document

You can start a new blank document by clicking the File tab and choosing the New command from the panel on the left in Backstage view. This opens the New screen, from where you double-click the Blank Document template to start a new document.

TIP! You can also open a new document using the keyboard shortcut Ctrl + N.

Task	Procedure
Open a document	• Click the File tab, choose Open, and navigate to your storage location. • Click the desired file, and then click the Open button.
Close a document	• Click the File tab and choose Close.
Start a new document	• Click the File tab and choose New, then double-click the Blank Document template. Or, press ⌑Ctrl⌑+⌑N⌑.

 HANDS-ON 1.7 **Start a New Document**

In this exercise, you will open a new blank document. No documents should be open in the Word window.

1. Click the **File** tab and choose **New** from the left-hand panel.

2. Double-click the **Blank Document** template to start a new document.
   Now you will close this new document and try using the shortcut keystrokes to start another one.

3. Click the **File** tab and choose **Close** from the left-hand panel.

4. Hold down the ⌑Ctrl⌑ key and tap the ⌑N⌑ key on your keyboard.
   Leave the document open.

Getting Help in Word

The Microsoft Word Help button appears in the upper-right corner of the Word screen and other Office 2013 applications. The Help window contains a search box, a list of popular searches, getting started aids, and online training options.

 HANDS-ON 1.8 **Use Word Help**

In this exercise, you will work with several Help techniques.

1. Click the **Help** ? button in the upper-right corner of the Word window.

2. Follow these steps for an overview of Word Help:

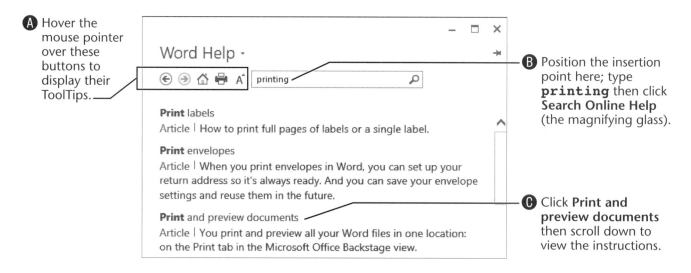

A) Hover the mouse pointer over these buttons to display their ToolTips.

B) Position the insertion point here; type **printing** then click **Search Online Help** (the magnifying glass).

C) Click **Print and preview documents** then scroll down to view the instructions.

Word Help

printing

Print labels
Article | How to print full pages of labels or a single label.

Print envelopes
Article | When you print envelopes in Word, you can set up your return address so it's always ready. And you can save your envelope settings and reuse them in the future.

Print and preview documents
Article | You print and preview all your Word files in one location: on the Print tab in the Microsoft Office Backstage view.

3. Take a few moments to experiment with Help. Try searching for **save** and **compatibility mode**. Feel free to explore any topics that interest you.

4. Click the **Close** ☒ button in the upper-right corner of the Help window.

Exiting Word

You exit Word and other Office 2013 applications by clicking the Close ☒ button in the upper-right corner of the window. If you have more than one document open, you need to close each document. It's important to exit your application in an orderly fashion. Turning off your computer before exiting could cause you to lose data.

HANDS-ON 1.9 **Exit Word**

In this exercise, you will exit Word. Since you haven't made any changes to your document, you won't bother saving it.

1. Click the **Close** ☒ button in the upper-right corner of the Word window.

2. If you are prompted to save your changes, click the **Don't Save** button.

3. If you have more than one document open, close any remaining documents without saving.

Word closes, and the Windows Desktop appears.

Concepts Review

To check your knowledge of the key concepts introduced in this lesson, complete the Concepts Review quiz here. Or, take the quiz online by going to the student resource center.

True/False Questions

			Page number
1. The insertion point automatically repositions when you navigate using the scroll bars.	**true**	**false**	_____
2. The mouse pointer looks like a white arrow when placed in the left margin of a document.	**true**	**false**	_____
3. The Quick Access toolbar contains commands for positioning the insertion point.	**true**	**false**	_____
4. Button arrangement on the Ribbon can vary depending on how the Word window is sized.	**true**	**false**	_____
5. The File tab provides access to file-management tasks, such as document saving, opening, and closing.	**true**	**false**	_____
6. Commands needed to create and edit documents are provided on the Ribbon.	**true**	**false**	_____

Multiple Choice Questions

7. Which shape does the mouse pointer have when it is in the text area?

Page number: _____

   a. Right-tilting arrow

   b. I-beam

   c. Left-tilting arrow

   d. Four-headed arrow

8. The Open dialog box is where you can _____.

Page number: _____

   a. save newly created documents

   b. convert documents created in older Word versions to Word 2013

   c. choose to start a new blank document

   d. navigate to and open previously saved documents

9. The Ribbon consists of three primary areas: _____.

Page number: _____

   a. tabs, groups, and the selection bar

   b. the Quick Access toolbar, commands, and groups

   c. tabs, groups, and commands

   d. the Quick Access toolbar, the status bar, and groups

10. When you add text to a document, _____.

Page number: _____

   a. the existing text moves out of the way to make room for it

   b. the mouse pointer is shaped like a white arrow

   c. the Mini toolbar appears in case you want to format text

   d. the existing text collapses to close the gap

Skill Builders

SKILL BUILDER 1.1 Identify Elements of the Word 2013 Window

In this exercise, you will name parts of the Word window. It's important to use the correct terms when talking about the Word program. If, for example, you need to discuss an issue with people in your IT department, they can help you faster if they are clear on what you are talking about.

1. Start **Word 2013** and click the **Blank Document** template.

2. In the table provided, write the correct terms for items A–G shown in the following illustration.

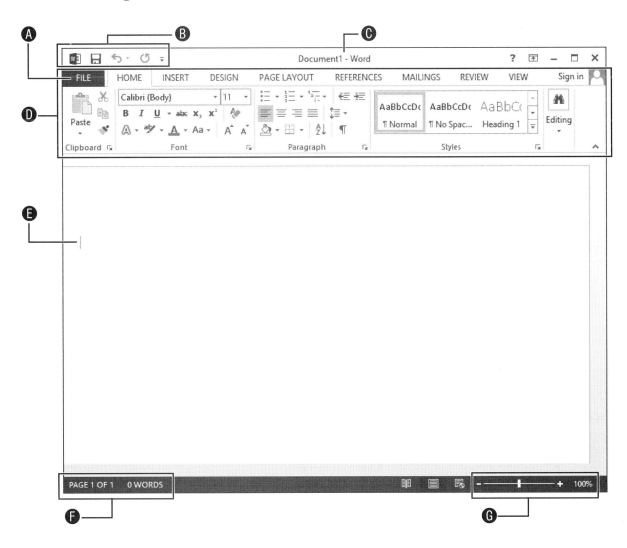

Letter	Term
A	
B	
C	
D	
E	
F	
G	

SKILL BUILDER 1.2   Use Word Help

In this exercise, you will use the Word Help window to find information that can assist you as you work.

1. Click the **Help** ? button in the upper-right corner of the Word window.

2. Click the **Keyboard Shortcuts** icon in the middle of the screen.

Keyboard shortcuts

3. Scroll through the window to see the many categories of keyboard shortcuts.

   When you become a Word whiz, you may want to learn about more keyboard shortcuts.

4. Click the **Back** ⊖ button in the upper-left corner of the Help window to return to the main Help window.

5. Click in the search box, type **table**, and tap Enter.

   You'll work with Word tables later in the course, so this will give you a glimpse into the future.

6. Click the **Insert a table** link.

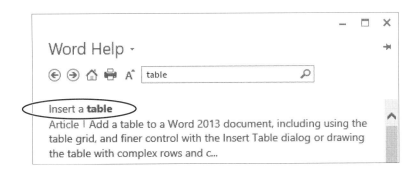

7. Scroll down the window to get a feel for some of the Ribbon commands you will work with.

8. Click the **Use Large Text** A⁺ button in the upper-left corner of the Help window.

9. Click the **Back** ⊕ button in the upper-left corner of the Help window and notice that the text remains large.

10. Click the **Use Large Text** A⁺ button again, and the text returns to its original size.

11. Click the **Close** × button in the upper-right corner of the Help window.

SKILL BUILDER 1.3   Navigate in Word

In this exercise, you will use a report you created for your Oriental Languages class to practice navigating in Word.

1. Click the **File** tab and choose **Open** from the left-hand panel.

2. Choose your main storage device, which will likely be **Computer** 🖥.

3. If necessary, navigate to your file storage location and open your Lesson 01 folder.

4. Double-click the file named **sb-Heart Report** to open it.

5. Click the **scroll bar** below the scroll box twice to move down two screens.

6. Click the insertion point in the middle of the first line on page 2.

7. Drag the **scroll box** to the top of the document and position the insertion point at the beginning of the document.

8. Click the **Scroll Down** ⏷ button and hold the mouse button down for a few seconds to scroll quickly through the document.

9. Drag the scroll box back to the top of the scroll bar.

Navigate with the Keyboard

10. Tap the down arrow ⏷ key enough times to position the insertion point in the first line of the first paragraph on the second page.

11. Tap [End] to move the insertion point to the end of the line.

12. Tap [Home] to move to the beginning of the line.

13. Press [Ctrl]+[End] to place the insertion point at the end of the document.

14. Press [Ctrl]+[Home] to move to the top of the document.

    If you press and hold the arrow keys, the insertion point moves quickly through the document.

15. Press and hold the ⏷ key long enough to move the insertion point to the first line of the first paragraph on the second page.

16. Hold down [Ctrl] and tap [→] three times to move to the right, one word at a time.

Close the Document and Exit Word

17. Click the **File** tab and choose **Close** from the left-hand panel.

18. Click **Don't Save** if a message appears asking if you want to save changes.

19. Click the **Close** ⟨×⟩ button in the upper-right corner of the Word window.

Word – Writing a Letter and a Résumé

In this lesson, you will change line and paragraph spacing. You will type a letter using AutoComplete to add the date, and you will insert bullet points to draw the reader's attention to important items in your letter. You will also learn about Word Wrap and when to use the [Enter] key. Then you will use Word's Table feature to help you lay out a résumé. Finally, you will save and print your letter and create an envelope for mailing your letter and résumé.

LESSON OBJECTIVES

After studying this lesson, you will be able to:

- Work with spacing and AutoComplete
- Use Word Wrap and the [Enter] key to lay out paragraphs
- Use bullet points and create a table
- Save and print documents
- Type an envelope

Case Study: Crafting a Cover Letter and a Résumé

Victor Gomez just completed his degree in sales and marketing. He is now ready to begin his career! He is interested in a Customer Support position at Goodspeed Industries. Using Word 2013, Victor creates a professional-looking cover letter, and he uses Word's Bullets feature to point out pertinent information he wants to draw the hiring manager's attention to. He uses a table to organize his résumé.

February 10, 2013

Mr. Anthony Williams, Hiring Manager
Goodspeed Industries
456 Apple Blossom Lane
Windy Hills, CA 94491

Dear Mr. Williams:

Your ad for a Customer Support Representative in this Sunday's Chronicle caught my attention. I believe I can offer Goodspeed Industries a blend of skills and enthusiasm that will help you maintain a satisfied client base.

- Principles of good salesmanship and clear, effective communication skills have been the focus of my studies for the last four years.
- A double major in Sales and Communications demonstrates that I can take on above-average challenges and responsibilities. I am not afraid of hard work, which is demonstrated by my 3.9 grade point average.
- The positions I have held in student government demonstrate my leadership abilities and my interest in people's needs and challenges.
- To finance my education, I worked in a hospital call center where I demonstrated the skill to quickly gain rapport and to efficiently assist patients with their billing questions.

I am excited about starting my professional career, and I would a[...]
Goodspeed Industries' success. I will call you in the near future to[...]

Best regards,

Victor Gomez

Enclosure

Victor Gomez
123 Cherry Blossom Lane
Windy Hills, CA 94941
415-555-1212
victor@yahoo.com

Objective	A challenging career where I can use my sales and communications skills
Qualifications	• Proven ability to close sales • Superb communication and presentation skills • Ability to quickly gain client rapport
Education	• B.S. Sales and Marketing, Windy Hills University, 2013 • B.S. Communications, Windy Hills University, 2013 • 3.9 Grade Point Average
Computer Skills	• Microsoft Word, Excel, PowerPoint, and Access • Contact Management Software
Work Experience	• Waiter, family restaurant, summers during high school • Customer Support Assistant, Windy Hills Community Hospital, summers and weekends during college
Student Government	• Student Body President, Senior Year • Class President, Junior Year • Student Council, Membership Coordinator, Sophomore Year

Typing a Cover Letter

In this part of the lesson, you will type a cover letter. Later you will create a résumé and an envelope.

 TIP! If you Google *cover letter*, you will find many websites that provide good ideas for cover letters designed to grab the attention of a hiring manager.

Text is always typed at the flashing insertion point; therefore, you must position the insertion point at the desired location before typing. As you type, the insertion point moves along in front of the text.

Line and Paragraph Spacing

The default spacing in Word 2013 is 1.08, rather than traditional single spacing. It adds an extra 8 points (a little less than an eighth of an inch) at the end of paragraphs. Therefore, rather than tapping Enter twice at the end of a paragraph, you just tap Enter once and Word adds the extra spacing.

When you choose the Blank Document template on the Word Start screen or on the New screen, you are using the default 1.08 spacing.

Some documents typically require single spacing, such as business letters, reports, and proposals. Word offers these methods for applying single spacing:

• Single Spaced (blank) template
• Line and Paragraph Spacing button

Single-Spaced Template   Choosing the Single Spaced (blank) template from the Word Start screen or from the New screen opens a single-spaced document. This is a good choice if the majority of your document will be single-spaced. If you will use single-spacing in only part of your document, the Line and Paragraph Spacing button is a good choice.

Single spaced (blank)

Line and Paragraph Spacing Button   If you start a new document using 1.08 spacing and then decide you want to apply single-spacing to a portion of the document, you can choose the options indicated in the following illustration. You must select (highlight) the text to be single-spaced, or at a minimum, select the paragraph symbol at the end of the text. Paragraph symbols carry formatting in them.

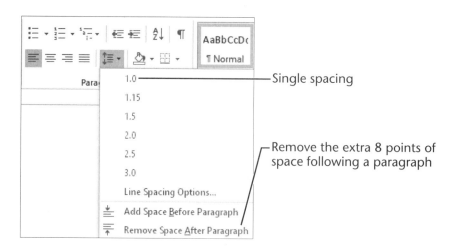

Apply these settings when you wish to type with more compact, traditional spacing.

Another way to eliminate extra spacing at the end of a paragraph is to press Shift + Enter rather than just Enter.

Nonprinting Characters

Word has a number of nonprinting characters that are not visible unless you turn on the Show/Hide feature. Nonprinting characters do not appear on the printed page even when the characters appear 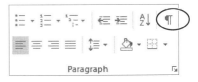 on the screen. The Show/Hide button on the Ribbon displays nonprinting characters.

The Enter and Spacebar keys, as well as several others, create nonprinting characters. Being able to see these characters can help you make sure the spacing is correct in your document.

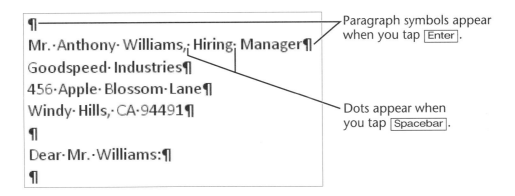

Paragraph symbols appear when you tap Enter.

Dots appear when you tap Spacebar.

Paragraph Symbols Carry Formatting All new blank documents contain a paragraph symbol; you need to turn on the Show/Hide feature to see it. Paragraph symbols carry formatting in them. For a new document based on the Blank Document template, the formatting includes default spacing of 1.08 lines and extra space at the end of a paragraph.

You can select (highlight) the paragraph symbol in a blank document and reformat it, thereby changing the default format for that document.

NOTE! Formatting paragraph symbols in this lesson provides a quick introduction to formatting. You will learn a lot more about formatting documents later in this course.

AutoComplete

AutoComplete can do some of your typing for you. It recognizes certain words and phrases, such as names of months and days of the week, and offers to  complete them for you. You accept the term that AutoComplete proposes by tapping Enter.

If you are typing a month with a short name, such as June, Word doesn't offer to complete the month. However, when you finish typing the month, Word offers to enter the full current date.

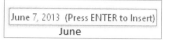

If you don't want to accept AutoComplete's suggestion, just keep typing and the pop-up note will disappear.

 HANDS-ON 2.1 Change Spacing and Use AutoComplete

In this exercise, you will display nonprinting characters, select (highlight) the embedded paragraph symbol, change the default line spacing to 1.0, and remove additional space after the paragraph. Then you will use AutoComplete to insert the date in a document.

1. Start **Word** and choose the **Blank Document** template.

2. Make sure the Word window is **maximized** ▫.

3. Follow these steps to turn on the Show/Hide feature:

A paragraph symbol now appears on the page.

Later in this book, such steps will be written as Choose Home→Paragraph→ Show/Hide ¶.

4. Follow these steps to select (highlight) the paragraph symbol:

Ⓐ Position the mouse pointer in the margin to the left of the paragraph symbol. (The mouse pointer should look like a white, right-tilting arrow.)

Ⓑ Click the left mouse button to select the paragraph symbol.

5. Choose **Home→Paragraph→Line and Paragraph Spacing** ↕≡.

6. Follow these steps to change the line spacing and remove the extra space after a paragraph:

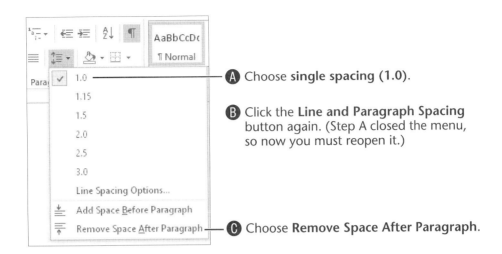

Ⓐ Choose **single spacing (1.0)**.

Ⓑ Click the **Line and Paragraph Spacing** button again. (Step A closed the menu, so now you must reopen it.)

Ⓒ Choose **Remove Space After Paragraph**.

Now you will enter the date using AutoComplete.

7. Tap ⌷Enter⌷ six times to place the insertion point about 2 inches from the top of the page.

8. Start typing **Febr** but stop when AutoComplete displays a pop-up tip.
    AutoComplete suggests the word it thinks you are typing and offers to complete it.

9. Tap ⌷Enter⌷ to automatically insert *February* into the letter.

10. Finish typing the date as **February 10, 2013**.
    If you make a typo, use ⌷Backspace⌷ or ⌷Delete⌷ to erase from the left or right of the insertion point, respectively, and then continue typing. You can also click the Undo button on the Quick Access toolbar to undo mistakes, starting with the most recent error.
    Leave the document open.

The Enter Key and Word Wrap

Tap the ⌷Enter⌷ key at the end of a short line that must remain short. The greeting line in a letter is a good example; it consists of a short line.

Dear Mr. Williams: ⌷Enter⌷

You also use the ⌷Enter⌷ key whenever you need to create blank lines, such as between paragraphs.

When Not to Use the Enter Key   When you type along a line and reach the right-hand margin, Word automatically wraps down to the next line. You *should not* tap Enter at the ends of lines *within* a paragraph. If you do, it can make your life very difficult when it is time to make editing changes. Just let it wrap!

 TIP!   As you complete the exercises in this lesson, the text on your screen may not begin a new line at the same location as the illustrations show. Don't be concerned; just let the text wrap at the end of the line. Use Enter only where indicated.

 HANDS-ON 2.2   Use the Enter Key and Word Wrap

In this exercise, you will use Enter to create blank lines. You will also use Enter to force the inside address lines and the greeting line to remain short, and then you will let Word Wrap take care of the line endings in the main paragraphs.

Don't be concerned if you see squiggly red or blue underlines. They indicate possible spelling or grammatical errors, which you'll learn more about later. If you know you made a typo, just use Backspace or Delete to delete it and keep typing.

1. Tap Enter four times to generate white space after the date.

Word inserts a fresh line each time you tap Enter.

2. Type this inside address and greeting line, tapping Enter where indicated:

Mr. Anthony Williams, Hiring Manager Enter
Goodspeed Industries Enter
456 Apple Blossom Lane Enter
Windy Hills, CA 94491 Enter
Enter
Dear Mr. Williams: Enter
Enter

3. Type the following paragraph, but don't press Enter until indicated at the end of the paragraph.

Don't be concerned if your line widths are not the same as that shown here. Word Wrap will take care of the line endings.

Your ad for a Customer Support Representative in this Sunday's Chronicle caught my attention. I believe I can offer Goodspeed Industries a blend of skills and enthusiasm that will help you maintain a satisfied client base. Enter

The Bullets Feature

Use of bullet points makes it easy for your reader to find pertinent information in your document. If you are writing to busy people, such as hiring managers, they will appreciate bullets that focus their attention on the significant points. You can use the Bullets feature located in the Paragraph group of the Home tab to quickly create bulleted lists.

Once you begin a bulleted list, tapping [Enter] generates the next bullet. When you have completed the list, tap [Enter] twice to turn off the feature.

 HANDS-ON 2.3 Add a Bulleted List to Your Letter

In this exercise, you will use bullets to draw the hiring manager's attention to the main points that demonstrate why the applicant is qualified for the job.

1. Choose **Home→Paragraph→Bullets** 🔘.

2. Type this paragraph:

   · **Principles of good salesmanship and clear, effective communication skills have been the focus of my studies during the last four years.**

3. Tap [Enter] to generate the next bullet.

4. Type these bulleted paragraphs, tapping [Enter] where indicated:

   • **A double major in Sales and Communications demonstrates that I can take on above-average challenges and responsibilities. I am not afraid of hard work, which is demonstrated by my 3.9 grade point average.** [Enter]

   • **The positions I have held in student government demonstrate my leadership abilities and my interest in people's needs and challenges.** [Enter]

   • **To finance my education, I worked in a hospital call center, where I demonstrated the skill to quickly gain rapport and to efficiently assist patients with their billing questions.** [Enter]

Your last [Enter] generated another bullet; a second [Enter] turns off the feature.

5. Tap [Enter] again.

   Now you're ready to finish the letter.

6. Type this paragraph and closing:

   I am excited about starting my professional career, and I would appreciate the opportunity to add to Goodspeed Industries' success. I will call you in the near future to see if we can schedule a time to meet. [Enter]
   [Enter]
   Best regards, [Enter]
   [Enter]
   [Enter]
   [Enter]

   Victor Gomez [Enter]
   [Enter]

Saving a Document

When you are working on a document, it is located in your computer's memory. Memory is *temporary* storage, meaning that if you lose power, your computer loses its memory. If this happens, you could lose information.

To avoid this problem, you will save your letter on a storage device, such as a USB drive or the hard drive inside your computer. These storage methods are permanent, meaning your data won't be lost in the event of a power failure. You should save frequently—every five to ten minutes is a good idea.

Save Compared to Save As

In Word, you can save a document by issuing one of two commands: Save or Save As. The first time you save a document, you use the Save As command. After that, when you make modifications to a document, you use the Save command to update the file on your storage device.

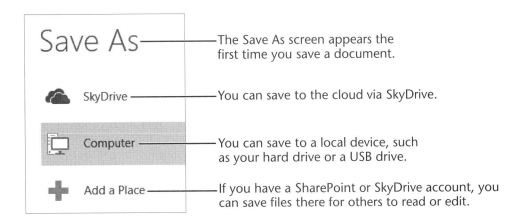

Save As——————The Save As screen appears the first time you save a document.

SkyDrive——————You can save to the cloud via SkyDrive.

Computer——————You can save to a local device, such as your hard drive or a USB drive.

Add a Place——————If you have a SharePoint or SkyDrive account, you can save files there for others to read or edit.

NOTE! Storing documents in SkyDrive is beyond the scope of this course. You will save your files on a local device.

After choosing a place in the Save As screen, the Save As dialog box opens. This is where you navigate to your file storage location, and name and save the file.

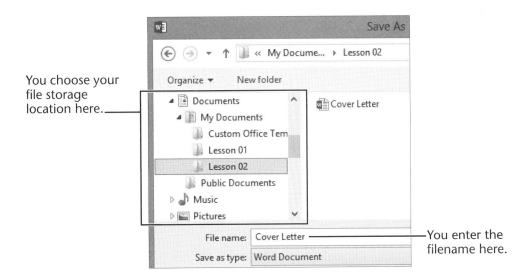

You choose your file storage location here.

You enter the filename here.

Word's DOCX File Format   A file format is a technique for saving computer data. Early versions of Word saved documents in the *doc* format. Word 2007 introduced a new file format: *docx*. Word 2013 uses the same docx format. This is important because users of earlier versions of Word cannot read Word files in the new docx file format without installing special software.

Users of early Word versions can download the Compatibility Pack from the Microsoft website in order to open, edit, and save files created in the new docx file format.

Save a Word 2013 Document in an Earlier Version   You can save a document created in Word 2013 in the earlier *doc* version if you want to share it with someone who uses Word 2003 or earlier. The Save As Type list in the Save As dialog box offers this option.

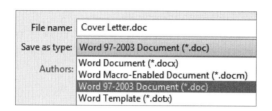

Displaying the *doc* or *docx* file format extension at the end of the filename is a setting you establish in Windows. Depending on your settings, you may not see extensions.

HANDS-ON 2.4   Save Your Cover Letter

In this exercise, you will save the cover letter you created in the previous exercise. This way, if there is a power failure, your letter will be saved.

1. Choose **File→Save As** to display the Save As screen in Backstage view.

2. Double-click the **Computer** 🖵 icon to open the Save As dialog box.

3. Follow these steps to save your document:

Your Save As dialog box may contain different files and folders than shown here.

A Use the Navigation pane to locate and open your Lesson 02 folder.

B Word always proposes a filename. Replace it with **Cover Letter**.

4. Click the **Save** button in the bottom-right corner of the dialog box.

Saving a Modified Document

The first time you save a document, you give it a name. If you make changes to the document after that, you must save it again so the changes are not lost. Once the document is saved and named, you can use the Save command rather than the Save As command.

You can use the Save button on the Quick Access toolbar or the Save command in Backstage view to save a modified document. When you use Save versus Save As, no dialog box appears; the saving just happens in the background.

 The Save button on the Quick Access toolbar.

QUICK REFERENCE: Saving Documents

Task	Procedure
Save a document for the first time	• Choose File→Save As. • Double-click an option (such as Computer) in the document storage pane, and then navigate to your storage location. • Type the filename and click Save.
Save a modified document	• Choose File→Save. Or, click Save on the Quick Access toolbar.

HANDS-ON 2.5 **Modify Your Letter and Save It Again**

In this exercise, you will add the enclosure notification to the bottom of the letter to notify the reader to check for an additional document in the envelope. Later in this lesson, you will create a résumé, which will be the enclosure.

1. If necessary, choose **Home→Paragraph→Show/Hide** ¶ to display nonprinting characters.

2. Position the insertion point at the bottom of the letter.

   Now you will add the enclosure notification to the letter. There should be a blank line separating the enclosure notification from the signature block.

3. If necessary, tap ⌈Enter⌉ to place the insertion point on the second blank line below the signature block.

4. Type the word **Enclosure**.

   Now you'll save the letter again to save the change you just made.

5. Click the **Save** button on the Quick Access toolbar in the upper-left corner of the Word window.

Printing a Document

You can print your document by choosing Print in the left-hand panel in Backstage view. Choosing Print opens the printer controls in the center panel (shown at left in the following illustration) and a preview of your letter in the right-hand panel.

Use this button to print.

Choose the number of copies to print.

Change printers or view a printer's properties.

Hover the mouse pointer over this symbol to learn how to specify which pages to print.

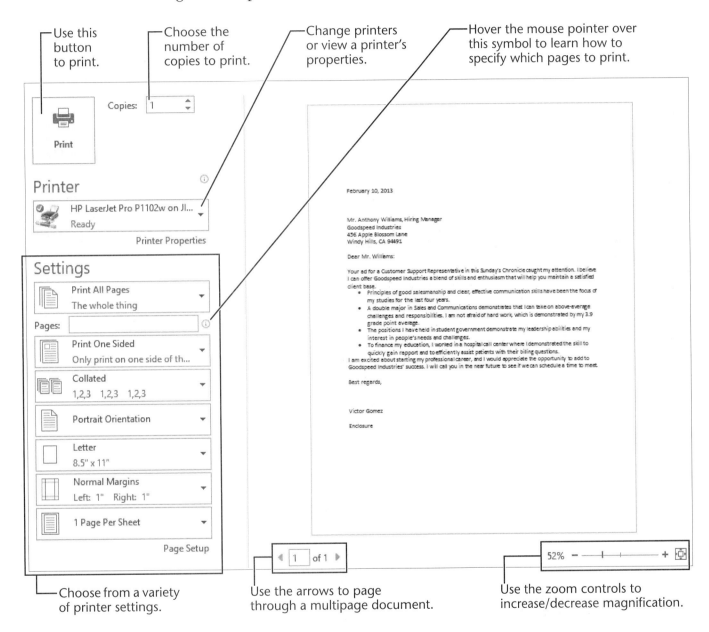

Choose from a variety of printer settings.

Use the arrows to page through a multipage document.

Use the zoom controls to increase/decrease magnification.

HANDS-ON 2.6 **Print Your Cover Letter**

In this exercise, you will preview your letter to see how it looks *before* you print. Then you will print your cover letter.

1. Choose **File→Print**.

2. Click the zoom controls and drag the slider in the bottom-right corner of the preview panel a few times to zoom in and out of the letter.

3. Click the **Zoom to Page** button to the right of the zoom controls to fit the page to the preview panel.

4. At the top of the Backstage view center panel, click the top part of the spin box once to change the number of copies to **2**.

5. Click **Print** at the top of the center panel to print two copies of your letter.

6. Choose **File→Close** to close your cover letter.

Using a Word Table to Organize a Résumé

A table is one of Word's most useful tools. Tables provide a powerful means of communicating information, yet they are flexible and easy to use. In this part of the lesson, you will use a table to create a résumé.

 TIP! If you Google *résumé*, you will find helpful guidelines for creating a résumé that's targeted to the job you are applying for.

Using the Table button on the Insert tab allows you to create a new table.

You drag the mouse pointer to select the desired number of columns and rows. The indicator shows your table dimensions (3x3 here).

Word's Live Preview feature shows what the table will look like before you insert it.

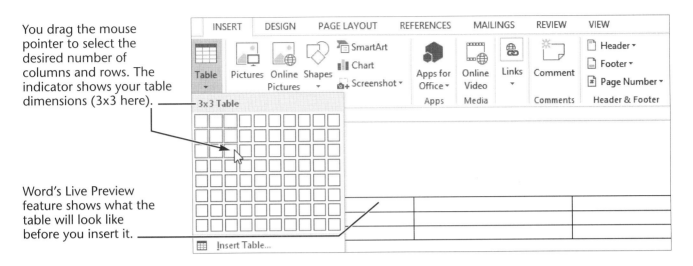

The rectangles that make up the table are referred to as cells.

Merging Cells and Centering Data in Cells

Frequently, the first row of a table contains a title describing the contents of the table. In the case of a résumé, it's likely the first row would contain the job applicant's contact information. Merging the cells and centering the information within that cell gives your résumé a polished look.

Victor Gomez 123 Cherry Blossom Lane Windy Hills, CA 94941 415-555-1212 victor@yahoo.com	
Objective	A challenging career where I can use my sales and communications skills
Qualifications	• Proven ability to close sales • Superb communication and presentation skills • Ability to quickly gain client rapport

Table Tools Contextual Tabs: Design and Layout Contextual tabs appear in context with the task you are performing. You will use the Table Tools' contextual Layout tab to merge and center-align the first row of the table.

Merge Cells —

Align Center —

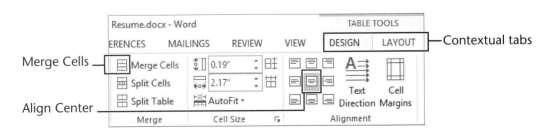

HANDS-ON 2.7 **Create a Table for Your Résumé**

In this exercise, you will create a table and then merge and center-align the cells in the first row.

1. Choose **File→New**.

2. Double-click the **Blank Document** template to open a new document.

3. Tap ⌷Enter⌷ four times so the table will be well-positioned vertically on the page.

4. Choose **Insert→Tables→Table** ▦.

5. Follow these steps to create a two-column, seven-row table:
   Remember, if you make a mistake, just click Undo ↶ on the Quick Access toolbar.

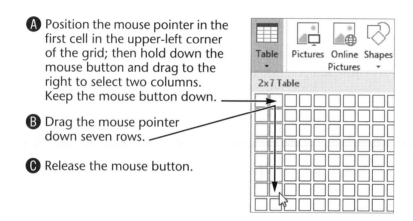

Ⓐ Position the mouse pointer in the first cell in the upper-left corner of the grid; then hold down the mouse button and drag to the right to select two columns. Keep the mouse button down.

Ⓑ Drag the mouse pointer down seven rows.

Ⓒ Release the mouse button.

A 2x7 table appears in your document. Now you will merge and center cells in preparation for entering contact information.

6. Follow these steps to merge and center the first row of the table:

Ⓐ Position the mouse pointer in the margin to the left of the first row of the table. (The mouse pointer appears as a white, right-tilting arrow.)

Ⓑ Click the mouse button to select (highlight) the first row.

Ⓒ The Mini toolbar appears whenever you select something in Word. Ignore it for now; it will fade away.

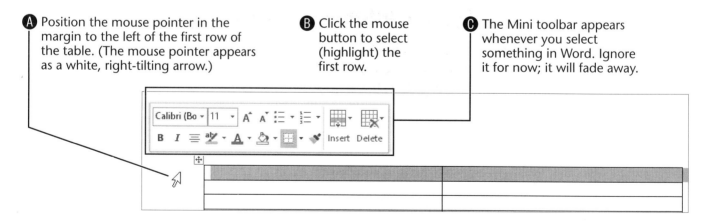

Notice the Table Tools with the Design and Layout contextual tabs that now appear on the Ribbon. They will appear whenever your table is active.

7. Choose **Table Tools→Layout→Merge→Merge Cells** ⊞.

8. Choose **Table Tools→Layout→Alignment→Align Center** ☰.

    If necessary, hover the mouse pointer over the alignment buttons on the left side of the Alignment group to display their ToolTips. Now when you type in the first row, the text will be center-aligned.

9. Click anywhere else in the table to deselect the first row.

Save Your File

10. Choose **File→Save As** to display the Save As screen in Backstage view.

11. Double-click the **Computer** 🖳 icon to open the Save As dialog box.

12. Navigate to your Lesson 02 folder, and notice that Word proposes a name in the File Name field at the bottom of the dialog box.

    You can replace the name that Word is proposing.

13. Delete the proposed name and type **Resume** to replace it.

14. Click the **Save** button in the bottom-right corner of the dialog box.

    Leave the document open.

Navigating in Tables and Adding Rows

You can position the insertion point in a cell simply by clicking it. However, it is often more efficient to use the keyboard to move among cells. You use the ⌷Tab⌷ key to move forward one cell and ⌷Shift⌷+⌷Tab⌷ to move back one cell. If the insertion point is in the last cell of the table, tapping ⌷Tab⌷ adds a new row to the bottom of the table.

Resizing Column Widths and Row Heights

Using the Table button grid to create a table inserts equally spaced columns. In many instances, such as when typing a résumé, you might prefer to vary column widths. Word's Table feature makes changing column widths a snap.

Row heights adjust automatically to fit the text you enter. The resize pointer appears when you place the mouse pointer on a column gridline. You can then adjust the column width by dragging the gridline left or right.

Dragging the resize pointer to the left narrows the first column.

The row height automatically adjusts to accommodate text entered.

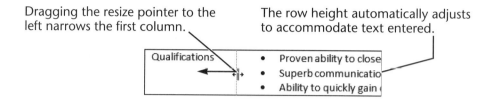

 NOTE! Make sure no cells are selected (highlighted) when you drag the column gridline. Otherwise, you might change the width of the selected cells only.

HANDS-ON 2.8 Adjust Column Widths and Enter Text

In this exercise, you will narrow the first column to accommodate the headings in your résumé. When you enter background information in the second column, you will see that the rows grow taller as you type. When you reach the end of the table, you will need to add rows. Not a problem. When the insertion point is in the last cell, you simply tap Tab to generate a new row.

1. Follow these steps to narrow the first column:

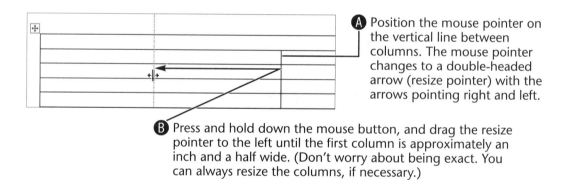

A Position the mouse pointer on the vertical line between columns. The mouse pointer changes to a double-headed arrow (resize pointer) with the arrows pointing right and left.

B Press and hold down the mouse button, and drag the resize pointer to the left until the first column is approximately an inch and a half wide. (Don't worry about being exact. You can always resize the columns, if necessary.)

Now you'll enter the contact information in the first row.

2. Click the insertion point in the first row.

3. Type **Victor Gomez** and tap Enter.

4. Type the rest of the contact information as shown, tapping Enter at the end of each line except the last line.

If your Show/Hide button is still turned on, you will see the paragraph symbols at the end of each line when you tap Enter. Feel free to turn Show/Hide on and off as you prefer.

Victor Gomez
123 Cherry Blossom Lane
Windy Hills, CA 94941
415-555-1212
victor@yahoo.com

---

5. Tap Tab to move to the first cell of the second row.

   Notice that when you tap Tab following Victor's email address, it becomes blue and underlined. This is an email link. If Victor were to email his résumé, the recipient could click the link to open a new email with Victor's email address in the To line.

   Now you will skip a row to add white space between the contact information in row one and the first line of the résumé.

6. Tap Tab two more times to move the insertion point to the first cell in the third row, and then type **Objective**.

7. Tap Tab to move to the next cell and type the following: **A challenging career where I can use my sales and communications skills**.

   The information should fit on one line and not wrap. But if it did wrap, don't worry. You can adjust the columns later. Again, you will leave a blank row so there's white space between the text entries to aid in readability.

8. Tap Tab three times to leave a blank row and to move to the first cell of the fifth row.

9. Type **Qualifications** and tap Tab to move to the second cell of the fifth row.

Add Bullets in the Table

Now you will add bullets to the information in the second column to make it easy for the recipient to locate the important points about Victor's background. You apply bullets in a table the same way you do in the rest of a Word document.

10. Choose **Home→Paragraph→Bullets** ⋮☰ to insert a bullet in the cell.

11. Type **Proven ability to close sales** and tap Enter.

    Tapping Enter generates the next bullet.

12. Type **Superb communications and presentation skills** and tap Enter to generate the next bullet.

13. Type **Ability to quickly gain client rapport** but don't tap Enter.

    You are now ready to move down two rows in the table.

14. Tap Tab three times and type **Education**.

15. Tap Tab again then choose **Home→Paragraph→Bullets** ⊟.

16. Type the information shown. Don't tap Enter after the third item.

> - B.S. Sales and Marketing, Windy Hills University, 2013
> - B.S. Communications, Windy Hills University, 2013
> - 3.9 Grade Point Average

Add a Row to the End of the Table

17. Tap Tab to add a new row to the table.

    When you use Tab to add a row, the new row takes on the formatting of the previous row—in this case a bullet appears in the second cell. But this row should be completely blank with no bullets, so you'll change that.

18. Tap Tab to move to the second cell of the row.

19. Choose **Home→Paragraph ›Bullets** ⊟ to turn off bullets in the new row.

20. Tap Tab to add another new row.

21. Type the rest of the information as shown. Remember to tap Enter to generate a new bullet; tap Tab to move from cell to cell and to add new rows at the end of the table. Turn bullets on and off as needed. Adjust the column widths to your satisfaction.

    Remember, click Backspace or Delete or use Undo ↶ if you make a mistake.

Computer Skills	<ul><li>Microsoft Word, Excel, PowerPoint, and Access</li><li>Contact Management Software</li></ul>
Work Experience	<ul><li>Waiter, family restaurant, summers during high school</li><li>Customer Support Assistant, Windy Hills Community Hospital, summers and weekends during college</li></ul>
Student Government	<ul><li>Student Body President, Senior Year</li><li>Class President, Junior Year</li><li>Student Council, Membership Coordinator, Sophomore Year</li></ul>

22. Click the **Save** 💾 button on the Quick Access toolbar in the upper-left corner of the Word window.

Removing Table Borders

The table borders make it easy to see where you are working as you add text to a table; however, a résumé might look sleeker without table borders. You'll use the Borders button in the Table Styles group of the Design tab to remove the table borders.

You click the menu button ▾ on the Borders button to open the menu. Clicking directly on the button face applies the border style that was last chosen from the menu.

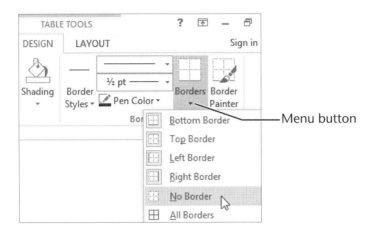

 HANDS-ON 2.9 **Remove Table Borders and Print Your Résumé**

In this exercise, you will remove the borders from the table. Then you will print the résumé.

1. Position the mouse pointer in the margin to the left of the first row of the table.

2. Press and hold the mouse button down and drag down in the margin to the last row of the table.
   This selects the entire table.

3. Choose **Table Tools→Design→Borders→Borders** ▦ **menu button** ▾ to display the border choices.

4. Choose **No Border** from the menu.
   The dotted grid lines are visible by default, but they are not the same as borders. They will not print. Now you will print your résumé.

5. Choose **File→Print**.

6. Click the **Print** 🖶 button in the Backstage view center panel.

7. Save and close your file.

Creating an Envelope

Word makes creating envelopes easy. You type the recipient's address and your return address in the Envelopes and Labels dialog box. If you attach the envelope to a letter with an inside address, Word will use the inside address to automatically fill in the delivery address.

The recipient's address goes in the Delivery Address field.

The Return Address goes here.

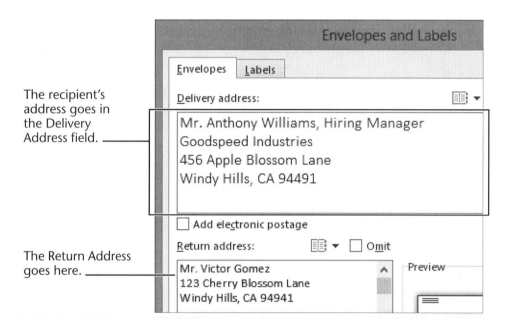

 HANDS-ON 2.10 **Type an Envelope**

In this exercise, you will type an envelope so Victor can send his résumé to the hiring manager at Goodspeed Industries. You will attach an envelope to your cover letter.

1. Choose **File→Open** and navigate to your file storage location.

2. Open your **Cover Letter** file.

3. Choose **Mailings→Create→Envelopes** .

   The Envelopes and Labels dialog box appears. Word recognized the inside address as the delivery address and automatically filled it in for you.

4. If an address appears in the Return Address box, tap Delete or Backspace to remove it.

5. If a checkmark appears in the Omit checkbox above the Return Address box, click the checkbox to remove it.

6. Click in the **Return Address** field and type this address:

   ```
   Mr. Victor Gomez
   123 Cherry Blossom Lane
   Windy Hills, CA 94941
   ```

7. Click the **Add to Document** button at the bottom of the dialog box.

8. Click **No** when prompted to save the return address.

9. Scroll down and notice that the envelope is attached to the cover letter.

   If you are not familiar with printing envelopes, you should consult your printer manual. The steps for loading and printing envelopes can vary from printer to printer.

10. Choose **File→Print**.

    In this example, you would choose *Print Current Page* from the button below. This would prevent the cover letter from printing again.

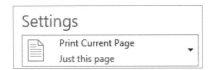

11. In this example, you will bypass printing the envelope.

12. Click the **Save** command in the panel on the left, and then close the file.

Concepts Review

To check your knowledge of the key concepts introduced in this lesson, complete the Concepts Review quiz here. Or, take the quiz online by going to the student resource center.

True/False Questions

				Page number
1.	Word Wrap keeps certain lines, such as a greeting line in a letter, short.	**true**	**false**	_____
2.	You made a change to a letter after saving and naming it. To save the new change, you must choose Save As.	**true**	**false**	_____
3.	You can use Enter to create blank lines in a document, such as the blank lines following the date in a letter.	**true**	**false**	_____
4.	You use the Show/Hide ¶ button to display and hide nonprinting characters.	**true**	**false**	_____
5.	AutoComplete recognizes certain words, such as names of months and days of the week.	**true**	**false**	_____
6.	You should not use Enter to end lines *within* a paragraph.	**true**	**false**	_____

Multiple Choice Questions

7. The default (preassigned) line spacing in Word 2013 is _____.

   Page number: _____

   a. 1.0

   b. 1.15

   c. 1.08

   d. 2.0

8. Which of the following is a characteristic of a Word table?

   Page number: _____

   a. It is made up of cells.

   b. It uses Word Wrap to navigate to the next row.

   c. You cannot adjust column widths.

   d. Live Preview does not work with it.

9. You can add a row at the end of a table by tapping _____.

   Page number: _____

   a. Tab

   b. Enter

   c. Ctrl

   d. Backspace

10. Which keystroke creates nonprinting characters?

   Page number: _____

   a. Enter

   b. PageUp

   c. Delete

   d. Shift

Skill Builders

SKILL BUILDER 2.1 **Write a Letter to a Friend**

In this exercise, you will conduct online research to find hints for writing a great résumé. Then you will send a letter to a friend who is looking for a job, sharing the information you've discovered. Since this is not a formal business letter, you will use Word's default 1.08 lines spacing.

1. Start a new document based on the **Blank Document** template.

2. Fire up **Google** (google.com) or the search engine of your choice.

3. In the Search box, type **hints for good resumes** and tap Enter.

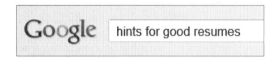

Ask your instructor for assistance if you are not familiar with web searches.

4. Make a note of four of the hints you think are most important.

5. Use these guidelines to type the letter that follows:

- Tap Enter six times so the letter is centered top-to-bottom on the page.
- Use AutoComplete to enter today's date.
- Let Word Wrap do its thing. Don't be concerned if your line widths don't match the illustration.
- Enter the information you found online after the bullets and in place of the word *Hint*.
- Use the paragraph symbols shown in the letter as a guide for when to tap Enter.
- Use Backspace or Delete, or Undo ↶ if you make a mistake.
- Save your letter in your file storage location as **sb-Letter to Martin**.

¶

¶

¶

¶

¶

¶

June·13,·2013¶

¶

Dear·Martin,¶

This·is·just·a·quick·note·to·let·you·know·that·I·have·done·some·research·lately·in·preparation·for·creating·
my·resume.·I·know·you're·working·on·your·resume·too,·so·I'm·sending·you·some·of·the·good·ideas·I've·
discovered.¶

   • → Hint¶
   • → Hint¶
   • → Hint¶
   • → Hint¶

Let·me·know·how·the·job·search·is·going.¶

Good·luck,¶

¶

Harold¶

Leave the letter open for the next exercise.

SKILL BUILDER 2.2 **Create an Envelope**

In this exercise, you will create an envelope and attach it to the letter you just typed.

1. Choose **Mailings**→**Create**→**Envelopes** ⬜.

2. If necessary, delete any address information in the Delivery Address box by tapping Delete or Backspace .

3. Type this address in the Delivery Address area:

Mr. Martin Nguyen
654 Willow Lane
Wheeling, WV 26003

4. If necessary, delete any information in the Return Address box.

5. If there's a checkmark in the Omit box above Return Address, click the checkbox to remove the checkmark.

6. Type this address in the Return Address area:

Harold Frost
789 Elm Street
Martins Ferry, OH 43935

7. Click the **Add to Document** button.

8. Click **No** when prompted to save the return address.

9. Save and close your file.

SKILL BUILDER 2.3   **Manage Your Mysteries with a Table**

In this exercise, you will keep track of your mystery novels that are on loan to your friends. You have quite a large collection, and keeping track of who has borrowed a book is becoming a mystery to you. You have decided to use Word's table feature to keep track of your books.

1. Start a new document based on the **Blank Document** template.

2. Choose **Insert→Tables→Table** ⊞.
The table grid appears.

3. Position the mouse pointer in the upper-left corner of the grid, and then hold down the mouse button and drag to the right to select four columns. Keep the mouse button down.

4. Drag the mouse pointer down six rows; release the mouse button.
A 4x6 table is created. Now you will enter the column headings.

5. Make sure the insertion point is in the first cell of the first row and type **On Loan To**.

6. Tap ⌷Tab⌷ to position the insertion point in the second cell of the first row and type **Title**.

7. Tap ⟨Tab⟩ again and type **Author**.

8. Tap ⟨Tab⟩ one more time and type **Main Character**.

9. Tap ⟨Tab⟩ to move the insertion point to the first cell of the second row and type **Brady**.

10. Enter the information shown, starting with the second cell in the second row:

On Loan To	Title	Author	Main Character
Brady	Caribbean Mystery	Christie, Agatha	Miss Marple
Opal	The Last Precinct	Cornwell, Patricia	Dr. Kay Scarpetta
Barbara	In the Last Analysis	Cross, Amanda	Kate Fensler
Madden	One for the Money	Evanovich, Janet	Stephanie Plum
Karl	Playing for the Ashes	George, Elizabeth	Thomas Lynley

Your friend, Lucy, just came by to borrow one of your mysteries. Now you'll need to add a row to the bottom of the table.

11. Make sure the insertion point is in the last cell of the table.

12. Tap ⟨Tab⟩ to add a new row to the bottom of the table.

13. Type the new row as shown.

Lucy	B is for Burglar	Grafton, Sue	Kinsey Millhone

14. Save the file in your file storage location as **sb-Mysteries on Loan** and then close it. Exit Word.

Word – Editing the Business Etiquette Column

In this lesson, you will learn techniques for selecting text; making editing changes; and using Undo, Redo, and AutoCorrect. You will use the Spelling & Grammar Checker, and you will move and copy text. Finally, you will learn to automatically find a word or phrase in a document and replace it with another word or phrase.

LESSON OBJECTIVES

After studying this lesson, you will be able to:

- Use a variety of techniques for selecting text
- Edit documents and use Undo, Redo, and AutoCorrect
- Use the Spelling & Grammar Checker
- Move and copy text
- Automatically find and replace text in a document

Case Study: Using the Spelling Checker and the Find Feature

Tyrone Williams writes a monthly business etiquette column for the *Windy Hills University Review* so graduating students can start thinking about human relations skills that are so important in the corporate environment. Tyrone finds Word's Spelling & Grammar Checker to be a great aid in helping him write an error-free column. The checker constantly monitors spelling, allowing him to correct errors as he types.

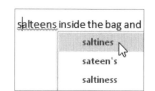

Word's Find feature allows Tyrone to move around quickly in his business etiquette column.

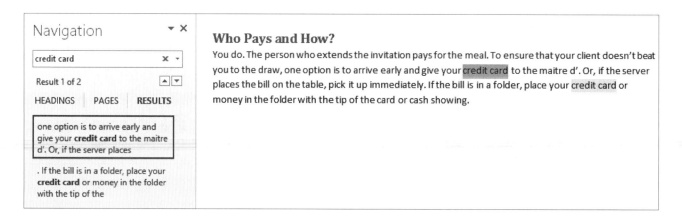

Selecting Text

In Word, you select (highlight) text in order to do something to it. For example, you select text before moving or copying it. You also select text when you want to replace or format it.

You work with two different areas of the screen when selecting text:

- The selection bar (in the left margin of a document)
- The typing area (between the margins)

When you select text, the Mini toolbar appears. You can ignore it in this lesson. The Mini toolbar contains commands for formatting text, which you will learn more about later in this course.

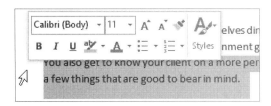

Selection Bar

The selection bar is in the left margin of a document. When the mouse pointer is in the selection bar, it looks like a white, right-tilting arrow.

The mouse pointer in the selection bar.

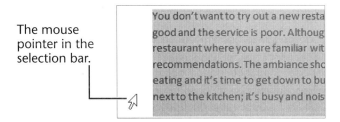

Typing Area

The mouse pointer looks like an I-beam I when you select text in the typing area, which is the area between the margins.

The mouse pointer in the typing area.

Selection Techniques

A primary method for selecting text is to click and drag the mouse pointer. In addition, Word provides mouse and keyboard shortcuts for selecting text. The following table lists several convenient text-selection shortcuts.

SELECTING TEXT

Item to Be Selected	Mouse Procedure
One word	Double-click the word.
Continuous block of text	Press and hold the left mouse button while dragging the mouse pointer over the desired text.

A line	Place the mouse pointer in the selection bar and click.
A sentence	Hold down ⎡Ctrl⎤ and click the mouse pointer in the sentence.
One paragraph	Triple-click anywhere in the paragraph, or position the mouse pointer in the selection bar and double-click.
Multiple paragraphs	Drag the I-beam over the desired paragraphs, or position the mouse pointer in the selection bar and drag to select.
Entire document	Triple-click in the selection bar, or press and hold ⎡Ctrl⎤ and click in the selection bar.
Nonadjacent areas	Select the first block of text, and then press and hold ⎡Ctrl⎤ while dragging over additional blocks of text.
Item to Be Selected	**Keyboard Procedure**
One word	Click at the beginning of the word, and then press and hold ⎡Shift⎤+⎡Ctrl⎤ while tapping ⎡→⎤.
Continuous block of text	Click at the beginning of the text, and then press and hold ⎡Shift⎤ while tapping any arrow key. Or, click at the beginning of the text, press and hold ⎡Shift⎤, and click at the end of the text.
A line	Press ⎡Shift⎤+⎡End⎤ to select from the insertion point to the end of the line. Press ⎡Shift⎤+⎡Home⎤ to select from the insertion point to the beginning of the line.
Entire document	Press ⎡Ctrl⎤+⎡A⎤.

 HANDS-ON 3.1 **Select Text**

In this exercise, you will select text from the selection bar and the typing area using both mouse and keyboard techniques. You'll start with the selection bar.

1. Start **Word** and choose the **Blank Document** template.

2. Choose **File→Open**, navigate to your Lesson 03 folder, and click **Professional Polish** to select it.

3. Click the **Open** button in the bottom-right corner of the dialog box to finish opening the file.

Select Text from the Selection Bar

4. Place the mouse pointer in the selection bar at the left edge of the screen just to the left of the first line of the first paragraph.

Most sales represent
people they like, and
You also get to know
a few things that are

The mouse pointer changes to a right-tilting arrow.

5. Click once to select the first line.

> Most sales representatives find themselves dining with their clients from time to time. People buy from
> people they like, and the dining environment gives your client an opportunity to get to know you better.
> You also get to know your client on a more personal level. To ensure a successful dining event, there are

The Mini toolbar appears when you select text. Ignore it for now; it will fade away.

6. Double-click in the selection bar to select the entire paragraph.

> Most sales representatives find themselves dining with their clients from time to time. People buy from
> people they like, and the dining environment gives your client an opportunity to get to know you better.
> You also get to know your client on a more personal level. To ensure a successful dining event, there are
> a few things that are good to bear in mind.

7. Triple-click in the selection bar to select the entire document.

If you find triple-clicking difficult, press Ctrl+A to select the entire document.

8. Position the mouse pointer in the typing area and click once to deselect (remove the highlighting).

Remember, clicking once in the selection bar selects an entire line. To remove *all* highlighting you must click in the typing area.

Select Text in the Typing Area

9. Position the mouse pointer over the word *Most* at the beginning of the first line of the first paragraph.

10. Double-click to select the word.

> Most sales representatives
> people they like, and the dir
> You also get to know your cl

11. Click once in the typing area to deselect the text.

12. Position the mouse pointer somewhere in the first sentence; hold down Ctrl and click.

This selects the entire sentence.

> Most sales representatives find themselves dining with their clients from time to time. People buy from people they like, and the dining environment gives your client an opportunity to get to know you better.

13. Click once in the typing area to deselect the highlighted text.

Select Text with the Keyboard

14. Position the insertion point at the beginning of the first line of the first paragraph.

15. Press and hold Shift, and then click at the end of the paragraph.

This selects everything from the insertion point to the Shift-and-click position.

16. Release Shift, and then click once in the typing area to deselect the text.

17. Position the insertion point at the beginning of the first paragraph again.

18. Press and hold Ctrl+Shift, and then tap → several times to select one word at a time.

19. Release Ctrl+Shift, and then tap any arrow key on the keyboard to deselect the text.

Leave the document open.

Editing Techniques

You know that the Delete and Backspace keys delete one character at a time. Word has several other ways you can edit text, including adding, deleting, and replacing selected blocks of text. Word will even help you edit with its AutoCorrect feature.

Add, Delete, and Replace Text

To add text to an existing document, simply position the insertion point where you want the new text to appear and begin typing. Word will make room for the new text as you type, while Word Wrap keeps the paragraph nicely organized.

You can delete a block of text all at once by selecting the text and tapping Delete. Word Wrap then closes up the gap and rewraps the text.

To replace existing text, select the text to replace and type the new text in its place. It doesn't matter if the selected text block is larger or smaller than the text replacing it. The surrounding text expands or collapses to accommodate the new text.

QUICK REFERENCE: Editing Text

Task	Procedure
Add text	Position the insertion point where you want the new text to appear and begin typing.
Delete text	Position the insertion point where you want to delete text, and then press Backspace (erase characters to the left) or Delete (erase characters to the right). Or, select a block of text and tap Delete.
Replace text	Select the text to be replaced, and then type the new text in its place.

AutoCorrect

Word has a wonderful feature called AutoCorrect that automatically corrects misspelled words and typos for you as you type. For example, if you type *aboutthe*, AutoCorrect changes it to *about the*. It corrects other errors, too, such as incorrect capitalization and accidentally typing with Caps Lock turned on.

 HANDS-ON 3.2 **Use AutoCorrect and Add, Delete, and Replace Text**

In this exercise, you will work with AutoCorrect and add, delete, and replace text. You will begin by adding a bullet point at the end of page 2. You will purposely make mistakes so you can watch Word automatically correct them for you.

1. Scroll down to page 2 and position the insertion point at the end of the last bulleted item.

2. Tap Enter to generate a new bullet.

3. Type **Turn offf** and tap Spacebar.
   Word corrects the word *off*.

4. Type **teh**, tap Spacebar, and watch Word change it to *the*.

5. Finish typing the bulleted item as shown:

Turn off the cell phone. You insult your guests when you indicate that your phone call is more important than they are.

6. Hold down ⌨Ctrl and tap ⌨Home to position the insertion point at the top of the document.

7. Position the insertion point at the beginning of the second sentence in the first paragraph.

> Most sales representatives find themselves dining with their clients from time to time. People buy from people they like, and the dining environment gives your client an opportunity to get to know you better.

8. Type this sentence:

Sharing a meal provides a more relaxed environment than the typical conference room.

9. Tap ⌨Spacebar.

Notice how Word makes space for the new text and how Word Wrap keeps things in order.

10. Follow these steps to select and delete text in the first paragraph:

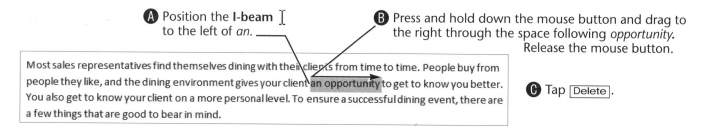

Ⓐ Position the **I-beam** I to the left of *an*.

Ⓑ Press and hold down the mouse button and drag to the right through the space following *opportunity*. Release the mouse button.

> Most sales representatives find themselves dining with their clients from time to time. People buy from people they like, and the dining environment gives your client an opportunity to get to know you better. You also get to know your client on a more personal level. To ensure a successful dining event, there are a few things that are good to bear in mind.

Ⓒ Tap ⌨Delete.

The insertion point should appear to the left of *to*.

> dining with their clients from time to
> t gives your client to get to know you
> o ensure a successful dining event, t

11. Type **a chance** followed by ⌨Spacebar in place of the deleted words.

Replace Selected Text

12. Position the mouse pointer over the word *perceive* in the first line of the second paragraph; double-click to select the word.

> Why? You don't want people to **perceive** that you
> the business lunch or dinner is all about business,

13. Type **think**.

The word you just typed replaced the selected word.

14. Save your document.

Spelling & Grammar Checker

Word helps you with your editing tasks. If you make a typo and AutoCorrect isn't sure how to fix it, the Spelling & Grammar Checker comes to the rescue. It monitors your spelling as you type and underlines words it suspects are misspelled with a squiggly red line. Right-clicking the underlined word displays a pop-up menu with suggestions of possible correct spellings. You only need to choose the correct spelling from the menu.

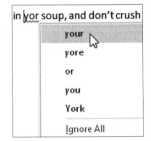

Grammar and Context Checking Word checks for possible grammatical and contextual errors and marks them with a blue squiggly underline. As you'll find with the Spelling Checker, you can ignore the underline, right-click the term and choose a replacement, or choose Ignore.

Sometimes the Spelling & Grammar Checker marks a word as a possible misspelling when it's correct. Some proper names fall into that category, although the checker has many common proper names in its dictionary and does not mark them. If Word marks a term incorrectly, you can either ignore the underlining (it won't print) or choose Ignore All from the pop-up menu.

Undo and Redo

The Undo and Redo buttons appear on the Quick Access toolbar. You've likely had a little experience with Undo by now. If you undo something and then change your mind, that's where Redo comes in. You can redo what you undid!

How Undo Helps You   Clicking Undo reverses your last action. If you click Undo again, the next-to-the-last action is reversed, and then the next-to-the-last from that, and so forth. Essentially, you are backing your way out of the problem. If you go too far or change your mind, just use Redo.

You can get out of most any catastrophe if you click Undo enough times. If you get into a mess, don't try to fix it; just undo it!

What Undo Can and Cannot Undo   Undo works for things you do that make modifications to a document: inserting text, editing text, formatting text, and so on. Undo cannot reverse actions like saving a document or selecting text. Once you close a document, it's too late to undo. If you want to make changes when you open the document again, you have to use editing techniques rather than the Undo feature.

 HANDS-ON 3.3   **Use the Spelling & Grammar Checker, Undo, and Redo**

In this exercise, you will purposely make some typos so you can see the Spelling & Grammar Checker in action. You will replace a word, and then undo the replacement, and then redo the action.

1. Press [Ctrl]+[End] to move the insertion point to the end of the document.

2. Make sure the insertion point is at the end of the last bullet point, and then tap [Enter] to generate the next bullet.

3. Type this sentence, taking care to purposely misspell *your* and *saltines*:
   Don't dunk bread in yor soup, and don't crush salteens inside the bag and dump them in your soup.

   Notice the squiggly red lines under *yor* and *salteens*, indicating possible spelling errors.

4. Place the mouse pointer over *yor* and click the right mouse button to display the pop-up menu.

5. Choose the correct spelling of *your* from the menu.

6. Now right-click *salteens* and choose *saltines* from the pop-up menu.
   Now you'll use Undo and Redo.

7. Press ⎡Ctrl⎤+⎡Home⎤ to return to the top of the document.

8. Double-click *representatives* in the first line of the first paragraph to highlight it.

> Most sales **representatives** find people they like, and the dining

9. Type **people** to replace the selected word.
   Hmmm, maybe *representatives* was better.

10. Click **Undo** ⟲ on the Quick Access toolbar as many times as necessary to return to the original word.
    Now you decide you prefer *people*.

11. Click **Redo** ⟳ on the Quick Access toolbar as many times as necessary to return to *people*.

12. Save your document.

Moving and Copying Text

When you move text, you remove it from its original position and place it in a new location. When you copy text, the original text remains intact and a copy is placed in the new location—it's in both places.

You can use the Cut, Copy, and Paste buttons in the Clipboard group on the Home tab to move and copy text.

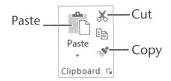

There are also handy keyboard shortcuts you can use to cut, copy, and paste. The following table describes the steps necessary to move and copy text.

QUICK REFERENCE: Moving and Copying Text

Task	Procedure (Ribbon)
Move text	• Select the desired text then choose Home→Clipboard→Cut.
	• Click the insertion point at the destination then choose Home→Clipboard→Paste.
Copy text	• Select the desired text then choose Home→Clipboard→Copy.
	• Click the insertion point at the destination then choose Home→Clipboard→Paste.

Task	Procedure (Keyboard)
Move text	• Select the desired text then press Ctrl+X to cut.
	• Click the insertion point at the destination then press Ctrl+V to paste.
Copy text	• Select the desired text then press Ctrl+C to copy.
	• Click the insertion point at the destination then press Ctrl+V to paste.

HANDS-ON 3.4 Move and Copy Text

In this exercise, you will move and copy text using both Ribbon and keyboard techniques. You'll start by moving the *Consider Various Tastes* paragraph above the *Eat Before Dinner* paragraph.

1. Position the mouse pointer in the selection bar to the left of the *Consider Various Tastes* heading, and then press and hold the mouse button and drag down through the last line of the paragraph.

> **Consider Various Tastes**
> Choose a restaurant that offers variety. Remember, your clients could have strict eating guidelines. Some will look for a low calorie offering on the menu. Others may prefer vegetarian dining, and religious differences can determine what people will eat.
>
>

2. Choose **Home→Clipboard→Cut** ✄.

3. Position the insertion point to the left of the *Eat Before Dinner* heading.

> **Eat Before Dinner**
> Why? You don't want people to

4. Choose **Home→Clipboard→Paste** 🗒.

   Now you'll use keystrokes to move the *Choose a Familiar Restaurant* paragraph above the *Eat Before Dinner* paragraph.

5. Position the mouse pointer in the selection bar to the left of the *Choose a Familiar Restaurant* heading.

6. Press and hold down the mouse button and drag down through the last line of the paragraph.

7. Press Ctrl+X to cut the paragraph.

8. Position the insertion point to the left of the *Eat Before Dinner* heading.

9. Press Ctrl+V to paste the paragraph in the new location.

Copy Text with the Mouse and the Keyboard

10. Scroll to the end of page 2 and place the insertion point at the end of the last bullet point.

11. Tap Enter three times to set off an area where you will copy information to.

12. Click and drag in the selection bar to select the first bullet point.

13. Choose **Home→Clipboard→Copy** 🗐.

14. Position the insertion point at the bottom of the page.

15. Choose **Home→Clipboard→Paste** 🗒.

    That information now appears in two places on the page.

16. Position the mouse pointer in the selection bar to the left of the second bullet point and click to select the line.

17. Press Ctrl+C to copy the information.

18. Position the insertion point at the bottom of the page.

19. Press Ctrl+V to create a copy of the information.

20. Press Ctrl+Home to move back to the top of the document.

21. Save your document.

Finding and Replacing Text

What do you do when you need to locate a specific word or phrase in a long document? Let Word locate it for you with the Find feature! There is also a Find and Replace feature, which is one step beyond Find. It helps you find existing text and automatically replace it with new text. As an example, this is a handy tool if you accidentally misspell a proper noun throughout a document. The Find and Replace commands appear in the Editing group at the right end of the Home tab.

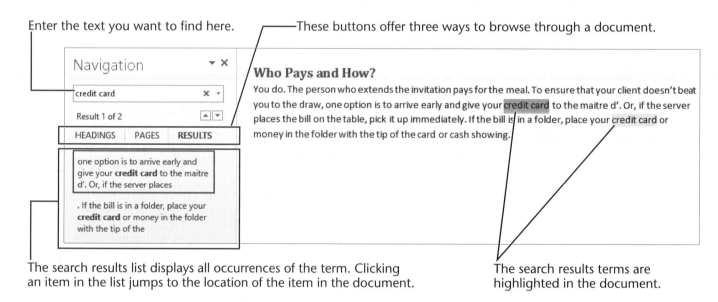

Find with the Navigation Pane

The Find command opens the Navigation pane on the left side of the screen. When you search for a term, the items found conveniently appear in the results list, giving you an overview of everywhere the term appears. Clicking an item in the search results list causes Word to jump to that location in the document. The search terms are also highlighted in the document.

Enter the text you want to find here.

These buttons offer three ways to browse through a document.

The search results list displays all occurrences of the term. Clicking an item in the list jumps to the location of the item in the document.

The search results terms are highlighted in the document.

The Find and Replace Dialog Box

The Replace option in the Editing group on the Home tab displays the Find and Replace dialog box, where you can enter the text you want to find and the replacement text. The following illustration shows the important parts of the Replace tab in the Find and Replace dialog box.

You type the term you want to find here. ⎯⎯⎯

You type the term you want to replace it with here. ⎯⎯⎯

Clicking the Replace button makes the replacement. ⎯⎯⎯

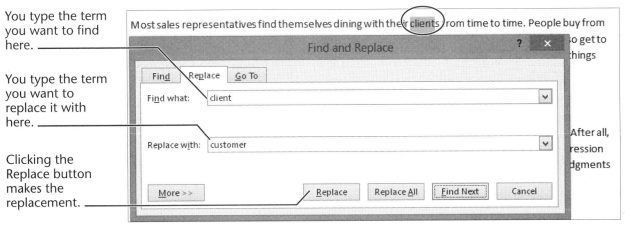

Although the search term is *client*, notice that Word found the plural form, *clients*. That's because the word *client* is embedded in the word *clients*. Word will make the replacement, maintaining the plural form when appropriate.

QUICK REFERENCE: Finding and Replacing Text

Task	Procedure
Find text	• Choose Home→Editing→Find then type the search term in the search box.
	• Click an item in the search results list to scroll the document to that occurrence of the term.
Replace text	• Choose Home→Editing→Replace then type the search term in the Find What box.
	• Type the replacement term in the Replace With box then click Find Next.
	• Click Replace to replace the first instance of the text or click Find Next to skip to the next occurrence of the search term. Or, click Replace All to make all replacements at once.

**WARNING!** Be confident about the changes that will occur when you use Replace All. If you are unsure, use Replace to monitor each replacement.

HANDS-ON 3.5 Use Find, and Find and Replace

In this exercise, you will use Find to locate the term *credit cards*. Then you'll use Find and Replace to locate the word *client* and replace it with *customer*.

1. Make sure the insertion point is at the top of the document.

2. Choose **Home→Editing→Find** to open the Navigation pane.

    > **⚠ TIP!** Click directly on the button face of the Find button. Clicking the menu button ▾ (the right side of the Find button) opens a menu, which you won't use in this lesson.

3. Type **credit card** in the box at the top of the Navigation pane.

    Both occurrences of the term appear in the search results list of the Navigation pane and both terms are highlighted in the document.

4. Click **Close** ⊠ in the upper-right corner of the Navigation pane to close it.

    Now you will find the word *client* and replace it with *customer*.

5. If necessary, position the insertion point at the top of the document.

6. Choose **Home→Editing→Replace** 🔡.

    The Find and Replace dialog box opens. Word remembers the last term you searched for and places it in the Find What field. You will just ignore it and type the new term you are searching for over the top of the old search term.

7. Follow these steps to begin replacing *client* with *customer*:

    Ⓐ Type **client** in the **Find What** box.

    Ⓑ Type **customer** in the **Replace With** box.

    Ⓒ Click **Find Next**.

    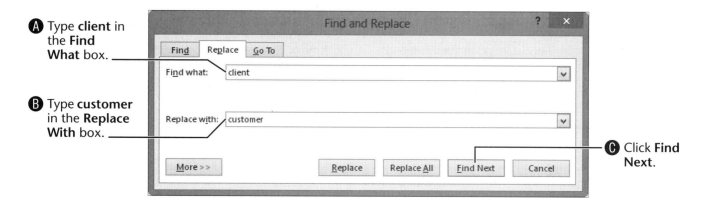

    Word highlights the first occurrence of the word. You may have to move the Find and Replace dialog box to see the highlighted word. If so, place your mouse pointer on the blue frame of the top of the dialog box, press and hold the mouse button, and drag the dialog box to a new location.

8. Click the **Replace** button at the bottom of the dialog box.

Notice that Word made *customer* plural like *clients*, which it is replacing. Word also highlights the next occurrence of the word.

9. Click the **Replace** button again.

10. Continue clicking **Replace** as each term is highlighted until you see a message indicting that Word has finished searching the document.

11. Click **OK** to close the message.

12. Click the **Close** button in the Find and Replace dialog box.

13. Save and close your document.

Concepts Review

To check your knowledge of the key concepts introduced in this lesson, complete the Concepts Review quiz here. Or, take the quiz online by going to the student resource center.

True/False Questions

1. You select text in order to do something with it, such as move or copy it. **true** **false** _____

2. When you use the Undo feature, you are essentially backing your way out of a problem. **true** **false** _____

3. When you copy text, the original text remains intact and a copy is placed in the new location. **true** **false** _____

4. When you delete a block of text within a paragraph, you must manually rewrap the lines using the Enter key. **true** **false** _____

5. When you use the Replace feature, Word always knows the correct replacements to make when you use the Replace All button. **true** **false** _____

6. The Find feature uses the Navigation pane to help you locate terms in your documents. **true** **false** _____

Multiple Choice Questions

7. The Spelling & Grammar Checker _____.

Page number: _____

  a. underlines misspelled words with a squiggly green line

  b. corrects all misspelled proper names

  c. is a subset of the AutoCorrect feature

  d. underlines misspelled words with a squiggly red line

9. The AutoCorrect feature _____.

Page number: _____

  a. automatically inserts the date

  b. is located on the Quick Access toolbar

  c. corrects line spacing

  d. automatically corrects misspelled words and typos

8. To select a single word with the mouse, _____.

Page number: _____

  a. triple-click it

  b. press Ctrl and click it

  c. double-click it

  d. position the mouse pointer in the selection bar and drag up or down

10. Undo works for _____.

Page number: _____

  a. things you do that make modifications to a document

  b. printing

  c. saving a document

  d. selecting text

Skill Builders

SKILL BUILDER 3.1 **Select Text and Use Undo and Redo**

In this exercise, you will select text using both the mouse and the keyboard. You will also use the Undo and Redo features.

1. Open **sb-Options** from your Lesson 03 folder.

Select Text with the Mouse

2. Place the mouse pointer in the selection bar to the left of the first main paragraph, and then double-click to select the entire paragraph.

3. Place the mouse pointer in the typing area and click once to deselect the text.

4. Select the paragraph again, but this time click and drag in the selection bar to select it.

5. Click in the typing area to deselect.

6. Double-click the word *option* in the first sentence of the first paragraph to select it.

7. Click in the typing area to deselect.

Select Text with the Keyboard

8. Click at the beginning of the *Interest Rate Options* paragraph.

9. Press and hold ⌐Shift⌐, and then click at the end of the paragraph to select the entire paragraph.

10. Release ⌐Shift⌐.

11. Tap any arrow key on the keyboard to deselect.

12. Click at the beginning of the *Interest Rate Options* paragraph.

13. Press ⌐Shift⌐+⌐End⌐ to select the entire line.

14. Tap any arrow key to deselect.

Use Undo and Redo

15. Hold down ⌷Ctrl⌷ and click the first sentence of the *Equity Options* paragraph to select the entire sentence.

16. Tap ⌷Delete⌷.

17. Click **Undo** ↶ on the Quick Access toolbar to undo the deletion.

18. Click **Redo** ↷ on the Quick Access toolbar to delete the sentence again.

19. Click **Undo** ↶ to undelete the sentence again.

20. Save your file and leave it open for the next exercise.

SKILL BUILDER 3.2 Move and Copy Text

In this exercise, you will practice moving and copying text. To begin, you will move the *Equity Options* paragraph above the *Interest Rate Options* paragraph.

Before You Begin: The sb-Options document should be open on the screen.

1. Select the *Equity Options* heading and its following paragraph.

2. Choose **Home→Clipboard→Cut** ✂.

3. Click in front of the *Interest Rate Options* heading.

4. Choose **Home→Clipboard→Paste** 📋 to move the text to the new location.

5. Scroll down to page 2.

Now you will copy text.

6. Select the *Interest Rate Swap* heading and its following paragraph.

7. Choose **Home→Clipboard→Copy** 📄.

8. Press ⌷Ctrl⌷+⌷End⌷ to place the insertion point at the end of the document.

9. Choose **Home→Clipboard→Paste** 📋 to place a copy of the paragraph at the end of the document.

10. Scroll to the top of the page and select the *Interest Rate Swap* heading and its following paragraph again.

11. Tap ⌷Delete⌷ to remove the original paragraph.

12. Save and close the file.

SKILL BUILDER 3.3 Add, Delete, and Replace Text

In this exercise, you will open a document and make editing changes to it. You will add, delete, and replace text.

1. Open **sb-Ripe Fruit** from your Lesson 03 folder.

   Locate the paragraph that begins with *Apples, bananas, avocados*…. This is where you will make the first few editing changes.

2. Position the insertion point between the word *tomatoes* and the comma in the first line of the paragraph.

3. Tap ⌑Spacebar⌑ and type this text: **(yes, tomatoes are fruits)**

4. Toward the beginning of the next line, double-click to select the word *vine* and type **plant** in its place.

   > Apples, bananas, avocados
   > will ripen off the vine. In fa
   > tropical fruits will ripen off

5. Toward the end of the third line, position the insertion point just after the word *yields*, tap ⌑Spacebar⌑, and type the this text: **(but is not mushy)**

6. In the second to last line of the same paragraph, position the insertion point between the word *gas* and the comma, tap ⌑Spacebar⌑, and type this text: **(ripening agent)**

7. In the last sentence of the paragraph, click to the left of the word *bag*, type **paper**, and tap ⌑Spacebar⌑.

8. In the first bullet point, double-click the word *broken* and replace it with **split**.

9. In the second bullet point, double-click the word *wrinkled* and replace it with **shriveled**.

10. In the second sentence of the fifth bullet point, place the insertion point between the word *pull* and the comma.

11. Tap ⌑Spacebar⌑ and type **off**.

12. In the last sentence on the page, double-click the word *usually* and tap ⌑Delete⌑.

13. Save and close the file.

Use Find and Replace

In this exercise, you will use Find to locate a term. You will also use Find and Replace to make changes to the document.

1. Open **sb-Energy Inspection** from your Lesson 03 folder.

2. Choose **Home→Editing→Find** 🔍 to open the Navigation pane.

3. Type **esl** in the search box at the top of the Navigation pane.
   Word locates the term in the document.

4. Click **Close** ☒ in the upper-right corner of the Navigation pane.

5. Make sure the insertion point is at the top of the document.

Use Find and Replace

6. Choose **Home→Editing→Replace** 🔤.

7. Type **offenders** in the **Find What** box and **wasters** in the **Replace With** box.

8. Click the **Find Next** button.
   The word *Offenders* is highlighted.

9. Click the **Replace** button to replace *Offenders* with *Wasters*.
   Word highlights the next occurrence of *offenders*.

10. Click the **Replace** button again.
    A message appears to let you know that Word has finished searching the document.

11. Click **OK** to close the message.

12. Type **recent** in the **Find What** box and **the latest** in the **Replace With** box.

13. Click the **Find Next** button.

14. Click the **Replace** button to replace *Recent* with *The latest*.

15. When the message appears, click **OK**.

16. Click the **Close** button to close the Find and Replace dialog box.

17. Save and close the file.

SKILL BUILDER 3.5 Use the Spelling & Grammar Checker

You're heading up a green construction project and are looking for volunteers to participate in the project. In this exercise, you will correct errors the spelling checker found in your project file.

1. Open **sb-Green Construction** from your Lesson 03 folder.
   Notice the misspelled words as indicated with the red squiggly underlines.

2. Right-click the word *Fluoorescent* in the sixth bullet point and select the correct spelling at the top of the pop-up menu.

3. Right-click the word *matterials* in the eighth bullet point and select the correct spelling at the top of the pop-up menu.

4. Correct the word *sustaainable* in the next bullet point.

5. Correct *Construcion* in the last line.

6. Save and close the file. Exit Word.

LESSON 4

Word – Encouraging Recycling with Flyers

In this lesson, you will create a flyer using character formatting, including changing the font type, size, and color. You will work with WordArt to convert ordinary text into graphic objects that you can manipulate with a variety of shapes and colors. You will use clip art to add interest to your flyers, and you will control the size and rotation of the images.

LESSON OBJECTIVES

After studying this lesson, you will be able to:

- Apply formatting from the Ribbon and Mini toolbar
- Use Live Preview and galleries
- Change paragraph alignment
- Work with WordArt and clip art images
- Create new folders for organizing documents

Case Study: Creating a Recycling Flyer

Suzanne Frost is a student teacher at a local high school. The Earth Sciences students are about to begin a recycling project, and Suzanne wants to create a flyer to attract the students' interest in the project. This is an opportunity to practice character formatting and to use some of Word's fun tools like WordArt and clip art.

Reduce, Reuse, Recycle

- Separate your trash
- Always look for recycle bins
- Reuse shopping bags
- If it's broken, fix it
- Buy recycled products
- Take along reusable cups
- Use washable napkins

Do Your Part!

Formatting with the Ribbon

Character formatting can help you get your message across. Examples of character formats include:

- Font type
- Font style
- Font size
- Font color

Character format settings take effect from the insertion point forward or until you change them. If you wish to format *existing* text, you must select the text first and then format it.

Fonts

The term *font* typically refers to character design, which can vary dramatically. You can apply any font in the Font menu to change the appearance of text.

This is an example of the Calibri font.

This is an example of Comic Sans MS.

This is an example of Old English Text MT.

This is the font that is in effect where the insertion point is positioned.

You can tell what a font looks like because its design is displayed in the font menu.

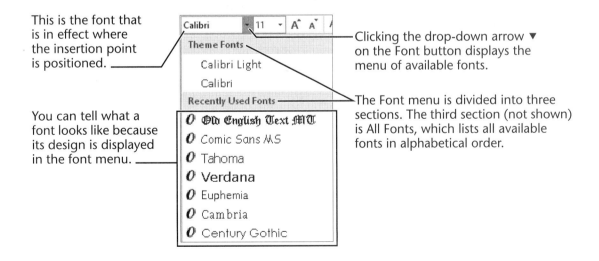

Clicking the drop-down arrow ▼ on the Font button displays the menu of available fonts.

The Font menu is divided into three sections. The third section (not shown) is All Fonts, which lists all available fonts in alphabetical order.

The Font Group

The Font group on the Home tab provides a convenient way to format characters. The following illustration points out some frequently used font attributes.

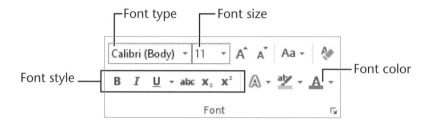

Font Size

Font size is measured in *points*, and there are 72 points in 1 inch. Frequently used sizes for typing body text (versus headings) are 10, 11, and 12 points.

Formatting with the Mini Toolbar

The Mini toolbar contains frequently used formatting commands. When you select text, the Mini toolbar fades in. After a pause, this shy little toolbar fades away. You can make it reappear by right-clicking the selected text.

In the following example, clicking the Bold **B** button on the Mini toolbar applies bold to the selected text.

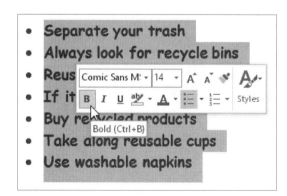

Using Live Preview with Galleries

Live Preview displays what a formatting change will look like without actually applying the format. In the following example, selecting a block of text and then hovering the mouse pointer over a font name previews how the text will look. Clicking the font name applies the font to the selected text.

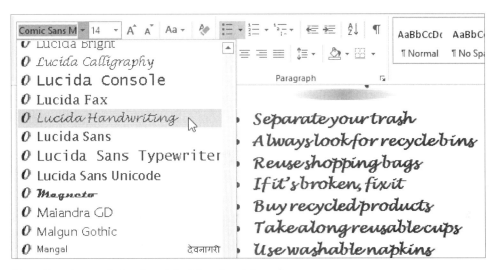

Live Preview of the Lucida Handwriting font

 HANDS-ON 4.1 **Use Character Formatting**

In this exercise, you will type recycling suggestions in your flyer. Then you will format characters using the Home tab's Font group and the Mini toolbar.

1. Start **Word** and choose the **Blank Document** template.

2. If necessary, choose **Home→Paragraph→Show/Hide ¶** to display nonprinting characters.

3. Tap ⎡Enter⎤ four times to move the insertion point down the page.

4. Choose **Home→Paragraph→Bullets** ⸬⁝.

5. Type this, tapping ⎡Enter⎤ at the end of lines when you need to generate a new bullet:

- Separate your trash
- Always look for recycle bins
- Reuse shopping bags
- If it's broken, fix it
- Buy recycled products
- Take along reusable cups
- Use washable napkins

6. Tap ⎡Enter⎤ three times to turn off bullets and add blank lines below the text. You're adding space because later you will add WordArt at the bottom of the page.

7. Now select the lines you typed.

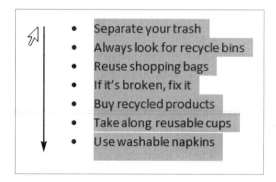

You will use Live Preview to explore a variety of fonts.

8. Make sure the **Home** tab is still active.

9. Follow these steps to use Live Preview:

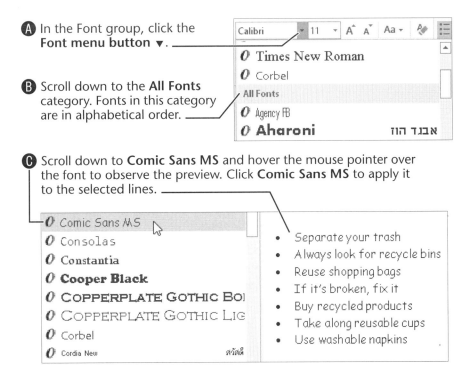

A In the Font group, click the **Font menu button** ▾.

B Scroll down to the **All Fonts** category. Fonts in this category are in alphabetical order.

C Scroll down to **Comic Sans MS** and hover the mouse pointer over the font to observe the preview. Click **Comic Sans MS** to apply it to the selected lines.

Now you'll change the font size.

10. Make sure the lines are selected, and then follow these steps to change the size:

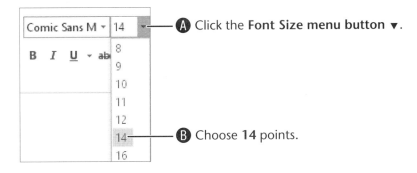

A Click the **Font Size menu button** ▾.

B Choose **14** points.

Apply Formatting Using the Ribbon and Mini Toolbar

The Bold, Italic, and Underline buttons toggle on and off. That is, you click the Italic button to apply the italic format, and you click the same button to remove the format. The same is true for the Bold and Underline buttons.

11. With the lines still selected, choose **Home→Font→Italic** *I*.

12. Choose **Home→Font→Underline** U.

13. Now click the **Italic** *I* button again to turn it off.

14. Click the **Underline** U button again to turn it off.

Next you will use the Mini toolbar to turn on the Bold feature.

15. Click in the document to deselect the highlighted text.

16. Select the lines again and notice that the Mini toolbar fades into sight.

17. Click the **Bold** B button on the toolbar to apply bold to the selected text.

Now you will apply color to your text with the Mini toolbar.

18. Follow these steps to apply a shade of green to the text:

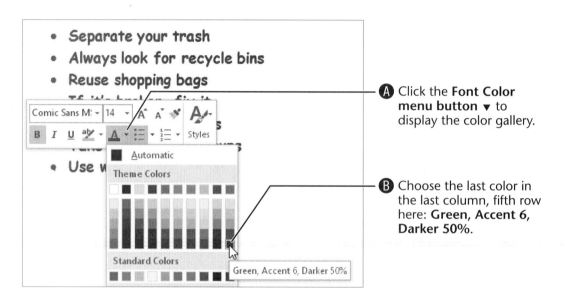

Ⓐ Click the **Font Color menu button** ▼ to display the color gallery.

Ⓑ Choose the last color in the last column, fifth row here: **Green, Accent 6, Darker 50%**.

Leave the file open.

Saving a Document to a New Folder

A folder is an electronic location where you store groups of related files. So far, you have been storing files in the folders that relate to a lesson, such as the Lesson 04 folder. You can even create folders within folders for organizing your documents. Creating folders is a simple matter with Word 2013. The Save As dialog box has a button for creating a new folder.

Naming Folders

When you click the New Folder button, Windows displays a New Folder. The *New folder* text is selected so you can just type your new folder's name over the top of the highlighted text.

There are certain naming rules you must follow when you create a folder. If you try to name a folder without following the rules, Word displays an error message. The following table lists the rules for naming folders.

RULES FOR NAMING FOLDERS

Rule	Description
Folder name length	A folder name can contain up to 255 characters.
Characters allowed in folder names	A folder name may contain alphabetic characters, numbers, spaces, periods, commas, semicolons, dashes, apostrophes, and parentheses.
Characters not allowed in folder names	A folder name *cannot* contain these characters: \ / : * ? " < >	

HANDS-ON 4.2 **Create a Folder and Save Your Flyer**

You know it's likely that you'll want to create more than one flyer for the recycling project. In this exercise, you will create a new folder specifically for saving flyers.

1. Choose **File→Save As**.

2. Navigate to your Lesson 04 folder and click the **New Folder** button at the top of the dialog box.

3. Type **Flyers** over the top of the highlighted *New folder* text and tap Enter.

4. Double-click the folder to open it.

5. Type **Recycle Flyer** in the File Name box at the bottom of the Save As dialog box, and then click **Save**.

Setting Paragraph Alignment

Typically, you use paragraph alignment to align text between the margins of a document. You can also use it to align clip art and other graphic images. Paragraph alignment buttons are located in the Paragraph group of the Home tab. Alignment options include Align Left, Center, Align Right, and Justify.

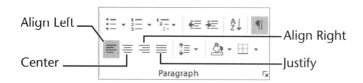

Align Left — Align Right — Center — Justify — Paragraph

ALIGNMENT OPTIONS

Alignment	Example	Alignment	Example
Align Left aligns text with a straight left margin and a ragged right margin.		Center centers text between the margins.	
Align Right aligns text with a ragged left margin and a straight right margin.		Justify aligns text with straight left and right margins. It typically appears in magazines and newspapers.	

 HANDS-ON 4.3 Set Paragraph Alignment

In this exercise, you will use the paragraph alignment buttons in the Paragraph group of the Home tab to align text between the margins.

1. Position the insertion point anywhere in a line of text.

2. Choose **Home→Paragraph→Center** ☰.
   The text is centered between the margins.

3. Choose **Home→Paragraph→Align Right** ☰.
   The text is now aligned with the right margin.

4. Choose **Home→Paragraph→Align Left** ☰ to align the text at the left margin.

Creating WordArt

WordArt is a graphic text image. You can format the image in a variety of shapes and colors. WordArt makes text look flashy—the perfect thing for a flyer. WordArt also makes interesting document headings.

 HANDS-ON 4.4 **Insert WordArt**

In this exercise, you will create a WordArt object by selecting a design from the WordArt gallery and typing the text that will appear in the object.

1. Press Ctrl + Home to position the insertion point at the top of the page.

2. Choose **Insert→Text→WordArt** 🅰.

3. Choose the fifth style in the second row of the WordArt gallery.

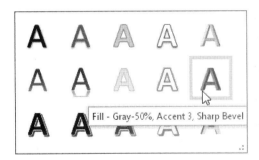

A text box opens so you can type the flyer heading. Notice the little square handles surrounding the object, indicating that it's selected. You'll learn more about that in the next topic.

4. Type **Reduce, Reuse, Recycle** in the text box.

Formatting WordArt

You can format WordArt in a variety of ways. For example, you can change the shape, apply a 3-D style, and add shadow effects. The following illustration shows an example of using Live Preview with the Bevel gallery to preview the formatting effect.

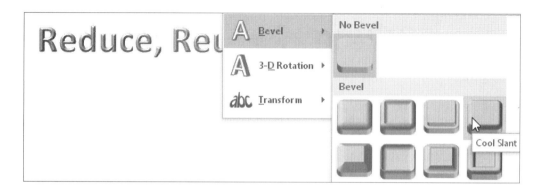

Contextual Tabs on the Ribbon

Contextual tabs appear in context with the task you are performing. When you select a WordArt object, the Drawing Tools' Format tab appears. Here you will find many features for formatting your WordArt.

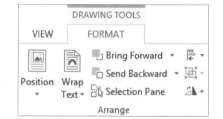

Selecting, Sizing, and Rotating WordArt

When you select a WordArt object, small squares known as handles surround it. When the insertion point is flashing in a word, only that word is selected; the box surrounding the object is made up of a dashed line. When you click directly on the line, it becomes solid, indicating that all words in the box are selected. Any formatting you do applies to all words.

The circular arrow at the top of the image is the rotate handle, which you can drag with the mouse pointer to rotate the image. You'll learn more about rotating images when you insert clip art later in this lesson.

When you position the mouse pointer on a handle, the pointer changes to a double-headed arrow, which you can drag to increase or decrease the size of the object. Sizing from a corner handle changes the length and width relative to their original proportions.

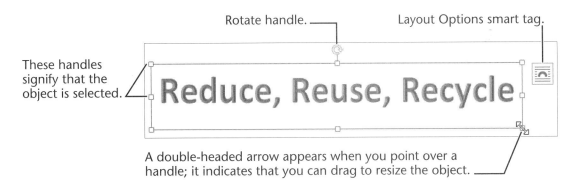

Rotate handle. ———

Layout Options smart tag.

These handles signify that the object is selected.

A double-headed arrow appears when you point over a handle; it indicates that you can drag to resize the object. ———

> **NOTE!** You will not use the Layout Options smart tag with WordArt. You will use it later in the lesson; just ignore it for now.

HANDS-ON 4.5 Format WordArt

In this exercise, you will use the contextual Format tab to test a variety of formatting options including applying a Bevel effect.

1. Click the border of the **WordArt text box**.

   The line changes from dashed to solid and the Drawing Tools' Format tab appears on the Ribbon.

2. Choose **Drawing Tools→Format→WordArt Styles→Text Fill 🅰 menu button ▾**.

3. Choose the fifth color in the last column: **Green, Accent 6, Darker 25%**.

   Your heading now blends with the bulleted text.

4. Choose **Drawing Tools→Format→WordArt Styles→Text Effects 🅰** to display text effect categories in the menu.

5. Slide the mouse pointer to the **Shadow** category, and then hover (don't click) the mouse over several options to see the effects in Live Preview.

6. Use the same technique to explore the other categories.

   Remember: Don't click until you decide which effect you will use.

7. Slide the mouse pointer to the **Bevel** category, and choose **Cool Slant** (last option in the first row).

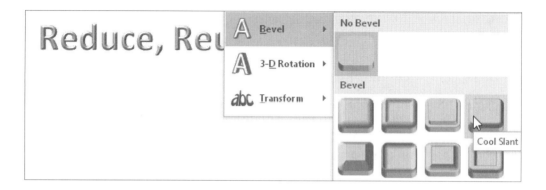

Now you will apply a Transform effect and resize the image.

8. Choose **Drawing Tools→Format→WordArt Styles→Text Effects** Ⓐ.

9. Slide the mouse pointer to the **Transform** category and choose **Chevron Up**.

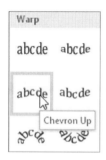

10. Position the mouse pointer on the square handle on the right side.
The mouse pointer changes to a double-headed arrow.

11. Press and hold the mouse button.
The pointer changes to a black cross.

12. Drag to the right until the right side of the text box is about an inch from the right edge of the page; release the mouse button.

Add Another WordArt Image

13. Press Ctrl+End to position the insertion point below the bulleted text.

14. Choose **Insert→Text→WordArt** 𝐴.

15. Click the last option in the first row: **Fill – Gold Accent 4, Soft Bevel.**

16. Type this text in the text box: **Do Your Part!**

17. Click the text box border to select the entire object.

18. Choose **Drawing Tools→Format→WordArt Styles→Text Fill** ![A] **menu button** ▾.

19. Choose the fifth color in the last column: **Green, Accent 6, Darker 25%**.

20. Choose **Drawing Tools→Format→WordArt Styles→Text Effects** ![A].

21. In the **Bevel** category, choose **Cool Slant** (last option in the first row).

22. Drag the right-side handle until the right edge of the text box is about an inch from the right edge of the page.

    This centers the text between the margins. Don't worry if the overall layout doesn't look right. You still need to add some clip art.

23. Save your flyer.

Using Clip Art

Clip art adds excitement to your documents. You can browse through your computer or other computers to locate images for your document, or you can search online for images. The Microsoft website offers a variety of royalty-free clip art.

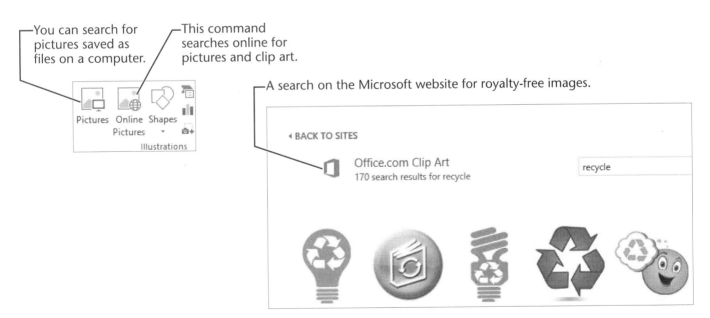

—You can search for pictures saved as files on a computer.

—This command searches online for pictures and clip art.

—A search on the Microsoft website for royalty-free images.

Rotating Clip Art

Clip art images have handles that work in a manner similar to WordArt handles. When you position the mouse pointer on a rotate handle, a circular arrow appears. You can then drag left or right to rotate the image.

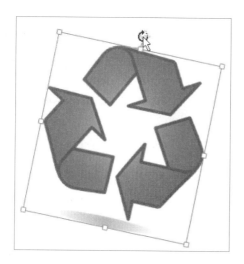

Resizing Clip Art

You can change the size of clip art objects by dragging on their handles like you did to resize a WordArt object. When you place the mouse pointer over a handle (other than the rotate handle), the pointer changes to a double-headed arrow. Then you drag to resize the object.

Resizing from a side handle stretches or squeezes an image as you resize it. Resizing from a corner handle changes the height and width proportionally.

 HANDS-ON 4.6 **Insert, Rotate, and Resize Clip Art**

In this exercise, you will search for a clip art image that's appropriate for the recycling project and place it in your flyer. Then you will rotate and resize the image.

1. Position the insertion point on the line below the flyer's heading.

2. Choose **Insert→Illustrations→Online Pictures** .

3. Follow these steps to search for clip art:

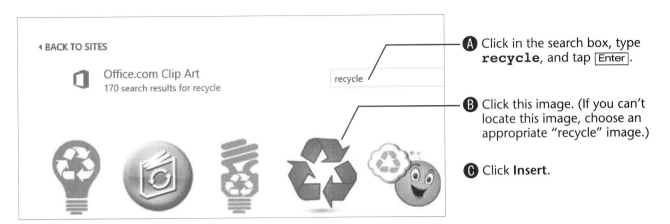

Ⓐ Click in the search box, type **recycle**, and tap Enter.

Ⓑ Click this image. (If you can't locate this image, choose an appropriate "recycle" image.)

Ⓒ Click **Insert**.

4. If necessary, click the clip art image once to select it.

The surrounding square handles are visible when you select the clip art object. Notice the rotate handle at the top of the image.

5. Position the mouse pointer on the rotate handle, press and hold the mouse button, and drag to the right to rotate the image as shown; release the mouse button.

6. Click **Undo** ↺ on the Quick Access toolbar to undo the rotation.

7. Position the mouse pointer on the lower-right corner handle. When the mouse pointer changes to a double-headed arrow, drag up and to the left about a half inch to make the image smaller.

If you chose a clip art image other than the one shown, the final image size should be approximately 2 ½ x 2 ½ inches. Don't be overly concerned about the size. You can modify the size to your satisfaction any time.

8. Save your file.

Layout Options

When an object is selected, a Layout Options smart tag appears to the right of it. Clicking the smart tag displays six text-wrapping options that determine how the surrounding text behaves relative to the object, such as square, top and bottom, and behind text. If text is wrapped around an image and the image is selected, you'll see an anchor icon that indicates the image is attached to text.

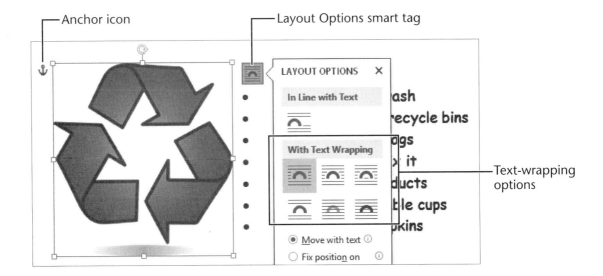
Anchor icon — Layout Options smart tag — Text-wrapping options

Cropping Clip Art Images

Cropping allows you to hide parts of an image. You simply choose the Crop tool and drag one of the image's cropping handles to hide the unwanted portion of the image. Cropping does not affect the original image. The area hidden by cropping is not deleted; you can un-crop an image if necessary.

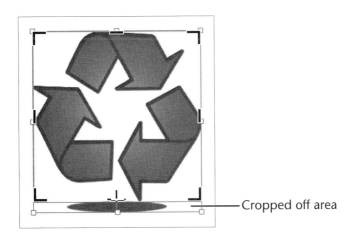
Cropped off area

HANDS-ON 4.7 **Wrap Text and Crop an Image**

In this exercise, you will use the Square text wrapping option with your clip art image, and you will experiment with Live Preview. You will crop an image, and you will center the image and align the text on the page.

1. If necessary, click the clip art image to select it and display the Layout Options smart tag.

2. Follow these steps to apply text wrapping:

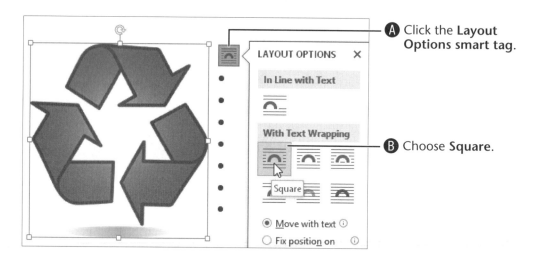

Ⓐ Click the **Layout Options smart tag.**

Ⓑ Choose **Square.**

3. Click in the document to view the effect of square wrapping.

   The image chosen and its sizing influence the wrapping effect. Now you'll position the image back in line with the text.

4. Select the object again, and then click the **Layout Options smart tag.**

5. Choose **In Line with Text.**

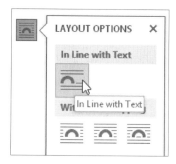

Crop and Un-crop the Image

Next you will crop the shadow from the bottom of the image. If you chose an image without a shadow, just clip a bit off the bottom of the image for the experience.

6. Choose **Picture Tools→Format→Size→Crop** .

7. Position the mouse pointer on the bottom-center thick, black handle.

The mouse pointer looks like a thick, black T-shape.

8. Press and hold the mouse button, and then drag up until the mouse pointer is above the shadow; release the mouse button.

9. Click in the document background to deselect the object, and observe the effect of the cropping.

You've decided you want to keep the shadow, so now you will un-crop the image.

10. Select the object again.

11. Choose **Picture Tools→Format→Size→Crop** .

12. Position the mouse pointer on the black bottom-center handle.

13. Press and hold the mouse button and drag down until you think the shadow will be visible again.

14. Release the mouse button.

If the shadow is not completely visible, readjust the image with the Crop tool until you can see the entire shadow.

15. If necessary, choose **Picture Tools→Format→Size→Crop** to turn off the Crop tool.

Now you will align the clip art image and the bullet points below it. You want the text to line up straight on the left, so you won't use the Center button, which would center each line between the margins individually. Instead you will use Tab to position the bullet points.

16. With the object selected, choose **Home→Paragraph→Center** .

17. Select all seven lines of text, and then tap Tab seven times.

When you select several lines of text, using the Tab key moves all of the lines at once.

18. Save and close the file.

Concepts Review

To check your knowledge of the key concepts introduced in this lesson, complete the Concepts Review quiz here. Or, take the quiz online by going to the student resource center.

True/False Questions

Page number

1. In the word-processing arena, font size is typically measured in points.

   true **false** _____

2. Live Preview shows how formatting changes look without actually applying the format.

   true **false** _____

3. Once you insert a WordArt image, you cannot change its shape.

   true **false** _____

4. A clip art image has a circular arrow rotate handle at the top of the image.

   true **false** _____

5. Word allows you to wrap text around a clip art image.

   true **false** _____

6. Paragraph alignment works for text but not for graphic images.

   true **false** _____

Multiple Choice Questions

7. You know a WordArt image is selected when _____.

Page number: _____

a. the handles are visible

b. it is highlighted

c. the WordArt task pane appears

d. it is visible from the Print command in Backstage view.

8. Which of the following is correct relative to cropping an image?

Page number: _____

a. Cropping hides part of an image.

b. Once you crop an image, you cannot recover the cropped portion.

c. You cannot crop clip art images that are from the Microsoft website.

d. The cropping tool is in the Layout Options smart tag.

9. Layout Options allow you to _____.

Page number: _____

a. keep typing in a paragraph without tapping Enter

b. wrap text around a graphic image

c. position the anchor icon

d. rotate a graphic image

10. The Mini toolbar _____.

Page number: _____

a. contains frequently used formatting commands

b. is located on the contextual Format tab

c. always appears at the bottom of the Word window

d. contains the Layout Options feature

Skill Builders

SKILL BUILDER 4.1 **Create WordArt and Format Text**

You are a teaching assistant in the Physical Education Department at Central College. The instructor heard that you are producing some interesting documents with Word, and she asks for your help. In this exercise, you will format the martial arts course description flyer that will be available when students sign up for classes.

NOTE! Turn the Show/Hide ¶ button on or off as you prefer.

1. Open **sb-Martial Arts Schedule** from your Lesson 04 folder.
   You'll use WordArt to format the first line of the document. Since the text is already typed, you can just select it and apply the WordArt style.

2. Select the first line in the document.

3. Choose **Insert→Text→WordArt** 𝐴 .

4. Choose the first WordArt style in the first row: **Fill - Black, Text 1, Shadow**.
   Now you will apply a text effect to the WordArt image.

5. Choose **Drawing Tools→Format→WordArt Styles→Text Effects** 𝐀 .

6. Slide the mouse pointer down to the **Glow** category and choose the third variation in the first row.

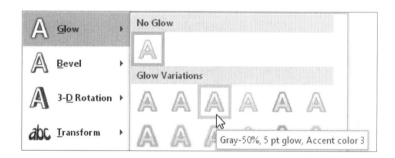

Now you will resize the WordArt image and add fill color.

7. Place the mouse pointer on the right-side handle and drag to the right until the department name is all on one line.

8. Position the mouse pointer on the border of the WordArt object (the mouse pointer appears as a four-headed arrow) and drag the object slightly to the left to center it between the margins.

9. Choose **Drawing Tools→Format→WordArt Styles→Text Fill** 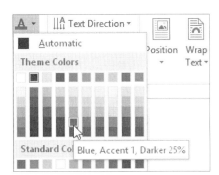 **menu button** ▼.

10. Choose the color in the fifth column, fifth row.

Format Text with the Ribbon and the Mini Toolbar

11. Select the lines *Fall Semester Schedule* and *Martial Arts Courses*.

12. Choose **Home→Font→Font Size menu button** ▼ and choose **16 point** font.

13. Choose **Home→Paragraph→Center** ≡.

14. Select the first course name, *Kung Fu Level 1*, and apply **12 point Tahoma** font.

15. Keep the line selected and right-click the selected text to display the Mini toolbar.

16. Click the **Bold** **B** button on the toolbar.

The toolbar remains open.

17. Click the **Font Color** **A** **menu button** ▼ and choose the color in the fifth column, fifth row, **Blue, Accent 1, Darker 25%**.

The Font Color button remembers the last color you chose from the menu, and that color appears on the button face. You can repeat the color without opening the menu. Just click the button face.

18. Format the other three course names using the same attributes: **12 point Tahoma** and the same shade of blue.

19. Select the first line below the heading *King Fu Level 1* and apply the **Euphemia** font.

20. Repeat the **Euphemia** formatting for the first line below the other three course headings.

21. Save and close the file.

SKILL BUILDER 4.2 Work with Clip Art and Create a Folder

It's time for the annual science fair where you are student teaching. In this exercise, you will help a student create a flyer to use as a handout for his project. You'll begin by inserting clip art.

1. Open **sb-Carbon Footprint** from your Lesson 04 folder.

2. If necessary, choose **Home→Paragraph→Show/Hide** ¶ to display nonprinting characters.

3. Position the insertion point next to the second paragraph symbol below the WordArt heading.

4. Choose **Insert→Illustrations→Online Pictures** .

5. Follow these steps to search for clip art:

A Type **bicycle** in the search box and tap Enter.

B Click this image. (If you can't locate this image, choose an appropriate "bicycle" image.)

C Click **Insert**.

6. If necessary, click the image to select it.
   Now you will resize, rotate, and center the clip art.

7. Position the mouse pointer on the image's top-right handle.
   The mouse pointer changes to a double-headed arrow.

8. Drag up and to the right about an inch to make the image a bit larger; release the mouse button. If you chose a different image, just resize it so it fits nicely on the page.
   Next you will center the image between the margins.

9. With the image selected, choose **Home→Paragraph→Center** .
   Now you will rotate the clip art. The circular arrow rotate handle is visible at the top of the image.

10. Place the mouse pointer on the rotate handle.

The pointer changes to a circular arrow.

11. Drag the handle to the right approximately the same degree as shown.

12. If any of the bullet points slip over to a second page, reduce the size of the image enough to place everything back on one page.

Save the Flyer in a New Folder

13. Choose **File→Save As**.

14. Navigate to your Lesson 04 folder and click the **New Folder** button at the top of the dialog box.

15. Name the folder **Science Projects** and tap Enter.

16. Double-click the folder to open it, and then click **Save**.

17. Close the flyer.

SKILL BUILDER 4.3 Use Layout Options with Clip Art

In this exercise, you will insert a clip art image in a document and experiment with wrapping text and positioning the image on the page.

1. Open **sb-Photographs** from your Lesson 04 folder.

2. Position the insertion point at the beginning of the first main paragraph.

3. Choose **Insert→Illustrations→Online Pictures** .

4. Follow these steps to search for clip art:

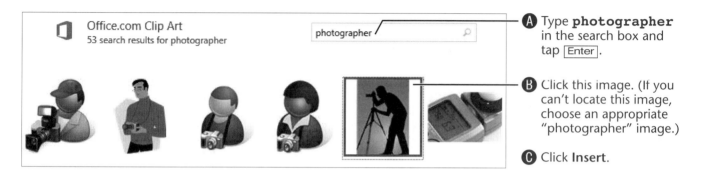

5. Resize the image to about a quarter of its original size. (If you chose a different image, size it to approximately 2 inches high by $1^1/_2$ inches wide.

6. Make sure the image is selected.

7. Click the **Layout Options smart tag** and choose **Square**.

8. Try out several other layout options, and then choose **Square** again.

9. Position the mouse pointer on the image's border (the mouse pointer appears as a four-headed arrow) and drag it to the right until it's positioned as shown.

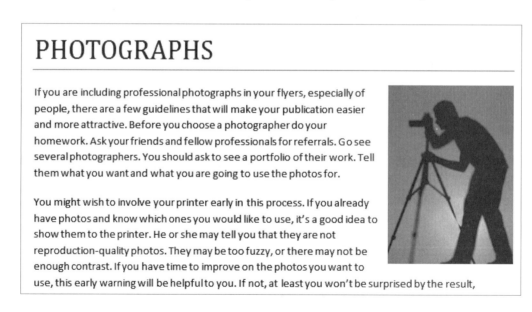

10. Save and close the file, and then exit Word.

Excel – Tracking Firefighter Training

In this lesson, you will learn the basics of Excel 2013. You will navigate in a spreadsheet and freeze data so it doesn't scroll off the screen. You will enter and edit data, and work with cell ranges. Then you will move, copy, and sort data. Finally, you will insert, delete, and resize columns.

LESSON OBJECTIVES

After studying this lesson, you will be able to:

- Identify important parts of the Excel window
- Navigate in a spreadsheet and freeze panes
- Enter and edit data
- Move, copy, and sort data
- Insert, delete, and resize columns and rows

Case Study: Creating a Training Database

You are an administrator at a fire department in your county. The chief has asked you to set up a training database for firefighters and emergency personnel. You find that Excel is a first-rate tool for the job. You realize that the ability to sort the database on any column is particularly helpful in organizing data in the various ways the chief requests.

Last Name	First Name	Hire Date	Rank	Shift
Alexander	Martin	3/24/1999	Firefighter/EMT-Paramedic	3
Bryan	Henry	3/13/1996	Firefighter	2
Cooper	Douglas	2/12/2013	EMT-Paramedic	2
Elizondo	Jose	1/27/1992	Firefighter/EMT-Paramedic	2
Ellis	Gregory	8/14/1992	Firefighter/EMT-Intermediate	1
Frost	Suzanne	5/19/1996	Firefighter/EMT-Basic	1

Sorted by Last Name

Last Name	First Name	Hire Date	Rank	Shift
Smith	Anthony	12/16/1991	Firefighter/EMT-Basic	3
Elizondo	Jose	1/27/1992	Firefighter/EMT-Paramedic	2
Ellis	Gregory	8/14/1992	Firefighter/EMT-Intermediate	1
Paulson	Glenn	6/15/1993	Firefighter	1
Jensen	Oliver	8/25/1994	EMT-Intermediate	2

Sorted by Hire Date

Last Name	First Name	Hire Date	Rank	Shift
Ellis	Gregory	8/14/1992	Firefighter/EMT-Intermediate	1
Paulson	Glenn	6/15/1993	Firefighter	1
Malik	Hasan	12/4/1995	Firefighter	1
Frost	Suzanne	5/19/1996	Firefighter/EMT-Basic	1
Morgan	Jack	8/1/1996	Firefighter	1

Sorted by Shift

Defining Excel

Excel 2013 is a spreadsheet (or worksheet) program that is part of the Microsoft Office 2013 suite of software programs. A spreadsheet program allows you to organize data in columns and rows, as well as to analyze the data and perform calculations on it. There are three kinds of entries in spreadsheets: text, numbers, and formulas.

You can use spreadsheets to create a variety of files, including income statements, financial statements, budgets, databases, and invoices.

Starting Excel 2013

- The method you use to start Excel depends on whether you are using the Windows 7 or Windows 8 operating system.

- **Windows 7**: Click Start , choose Microsoft Office from the All Programs menu, and then choose Excel 2013.

- **Windows 8**: Locate the Excel 2013 tile on the Windows Start screen; click the tile to start Excel.

Viewing the Excel Start Screen

The Excel Start screen is the first screen you see when you start the program. It offers several ways to begin working. Don't be concerned if your Start screen is arranged differently from this example. You can rearrange templates on the right side of the screen, and the appearance also depends on your screen's resolution.

You can begin by working on a recent workbook or by opening another workbook you saved earlier.

You can choose the Blank Workbook template if you're creating a spreadsheet from scratch, or you can use one of Excel's other built-in templates.

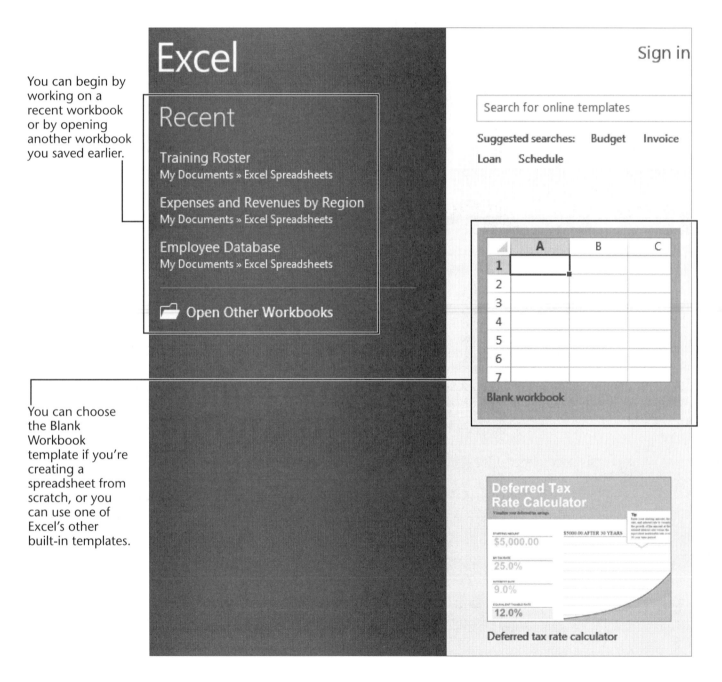

Excel

Recent

Training Roster
My Documents » Excel Spreadsheets

Expenses and Revenues by Region
My Documents » Excel Spreadsheets

Employee Database
My Documents » Excel Spreadsheets

Open Other Workbooks

Sign in

Search for online templates

Suggested searches: Budget   Invoice
Loan   Schedule

Blank workbook

Deferred Tax Rate Calculator

$5,000.00

25.0%

9.0%

12.0%

Deferred tax rate calculator

HANDS-ON 5.1A **Start Excel (Windows 8)**

Windows 7 Users: Skip this exercise.

In this exercise, you will start the Excel program.

1. If necessary, start your computer.

   The Windows Start screen appears.

2. Locate the **Excel 2013** tile.

3. Click the tile to start Excel.

   The Excel program loads, and the Excel Start screen appears.

4. Make sure the Excel window is **maximized** ▢.

5. Click the **Blank Workbook** template to open the Excel window.

 HANDS-ON 5.1B **Start Excel (Windows 7)**

Windows 8 Users: Skip this exercise.

In this exercise, you will start the Excel program.

1. If necessary, start your computer.

   The Windows Desktop appears.

2. Click **Start** 🔘 at the left edge of the taskbar and choose **All Programs**.

3. Choose **Microsoft Office**, and then choose **Microsoft Excel 2013** from the menu.

   The Excel program loads, and the Excel Start screen appears.

4. Make sure the Excel window is **maximized** ▢.

5. Click the **Blank Workbook** template to open the Excel window.

Exploring the Excel 2013 Window

Excel opens with a new blank workbook for you to enter and analyze data, and to maintain lists of information. There are a number of similarities between the Word window and the Excel window. For example, both windows have a File tab, a Ribbon, and a Quick Access toolbar.

The Suite Advantage

Now you're starting to see the advantage of working with a suite of software programs. When you learn one program, you're a step ahead when it's time to learn the next one.

Don't be concerned if your workbook window looks slightly different from the following example. The Excel screen is customizable.

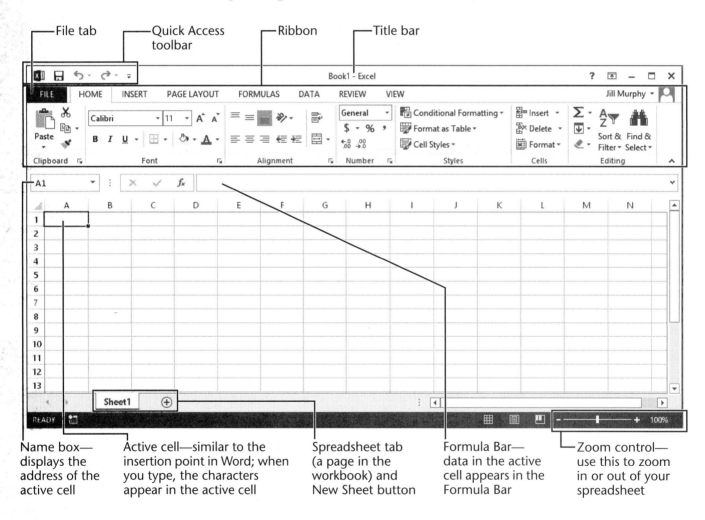

Name box—displays the address of the active cell

Active cell—similar to the insertion point in Word; when you type, the characters appear in the active cell

Spreadsheet tab (a page in the workbook) and New Sheet button

Formula Bar—data in the active cell appears in the Formula Bar

Zoom control—use this to zoom in or out of your spreadsheet

Workbook Organization

An Excel file is often referred to as a *workbook*. That's because, like a book, it's made up of pages. These pages are known as *spreadsheets* or *worksheets* (see the Sheet 1 tab in the previous illustration).

Spreadsheet   A spreadsheet is made up of a series of columns and rows. The columns are headed with alphabetic characters, and the rows are headed with numbers. There are 16,384 columns and 1,048,576 rows. (That's probably more room than you will ever need!) Since there are only twenty-six letters in the alphabet, when Excel gets to column Z, it starts over labeling the columns with AA, AB, AC, and all the way through AZ, and then to moves to BA, BB, BC, and so forth.

Defining Cells   A small rectangle appears wherever a column and row intersect. These rectangles are known as *cells*. All cells have addresses that are determined by the column and row indicators. The address of the first cell in the upper-left corner of the spreadsheet—in column A and row 1—is A1. A1 is the active cell in the following illustration; the active cell has a dark border around it. When you type data, it automatically goes into the active cell.

The address of the active cell appears in the Name Box at the left end of the Formula Bar.

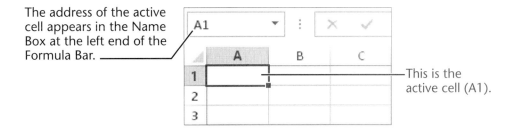

This is the active cell (A1).

Mouse Shapes in Excel

The mouse pointer in Excel takes on many different shapes, depending on what you are doing. Excel behaves differently relative to the mouse pointer shape. The following table describes the mouse shapes and their purposes.

EXCEL MOUSE POINTER SHAPES

Mouse Shape	Purpose
⊹	The thick white cross appears when the pointer is over a cell. Clicking the white cross pointer selects a cell. Clicking and dragging the white cross pointer selects a range of cells.
✛	The AutoFill shape appears when you place the mouse pointer on the tiny square (fill handle) in the bottom-right corner of a selected cell. Dragging the fill handle either copies cells or generates a data series to adjacent cells.
⇖	The mouse pointer looks like a white arrow when you move it over the Ribbon or when you use the scroll bars.
⊹⇖	The move pointer appears when you hover the mouse pointer over the edge of a cell or a range of selected cells (except in the bottom-right corner). You can then click and drag to move cells to a new location.
↔	The mouse pointer changes to the resize pointer when you place it between row or column headers. You can then click and drag to change the size of rows or columns. Or, double-click when the mouse pointer is between columns to make the column as wide as its widest entry.
⇨	When the mouse pointer is on a row header, it changes to a right-pointing arrow, which, when clicked, selects the entire row.
⇩	Placing the mouse pointer on a column header changes the pointer to a down-pointing arrow, which you can click to select the entire column.
I	The I-beam appears when you are entering or editing text in the Formula Bar or within a cell.

Navigating in an Excel Spreadsheet

If you are working with a large spreadsheet, it's convenient to know some techniques for moving around quickly. There are a number of mouse moves and keyboard techniques you can use. Some of them are the same as those used in Word.

Navigating with the Scroll Bars

When you navigate with scroll bars, the active cell does not move. After scrolling, you must click in the spreadsheet to reposition the active cell. You can see from the following illustration that scrolling in Excel is similar to scrolling in Word.

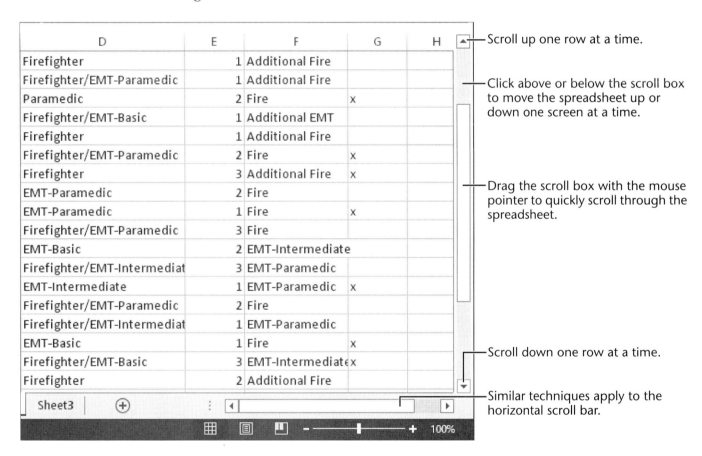

D	E	F	G	H	
Firefighter	1	Additional Fire			Scroll up one row at a time.
Firefighter/EMT-Paramedic	1	Additional Fire			
Paramedic	2	Fire	x		Click above or below the scroll box to move the spreadsheet up or down one screen at a time.
Firefighter/EMT-Basic	1	Additional EMT			
Firefighter	1	Additional Fire			
Firefighter/EMT-Paramedic	2	Fire	x		
Firefighter	3	Additional Fire	x		
EMT-Paramedic	2	Fire			Drag the scroll box with the mouse pointer to quickly scroll through the spreadsheet.
EMT-Paramedic	1	Fire	x		
Firefighter/EMT-Paramedic	3	Fire			
EMT-Basic	2	EMT-Intermediate			
Firefighter/EMT-Intermediat	3	EMT-Paramedic			
EMT-Intermediate	1	EMT-Paramedic	x		
Firefighter/EMT-Paramedic	2	Fire			
Firefighter/EMT-Intermediat	1	EMT-Paramedic			
EMT-Basic	1	Fire	x		Scroll down one row at a time.
Firefighter/EMT-Basic	3	EMT-Intermediatex			
Firefighter	2	Additional Fire			Similar techniques apply to the horizontal scroll bar.

Sheet3 (+) ◀ ▶

⊞ ▣ ▥ − ▬ + 100%

HANDS-ON 5.2 **Scroll in a Spreadsheet**

In this exercise, you will open a workbook and scroll around in a spreadsheet.

1. Choose **File→Open**.

2. Navigate to the Lesson 05 folder and open **Training Roster**.

3. Follow these steps to use the scroll bar to navigate in the spreadsheet:

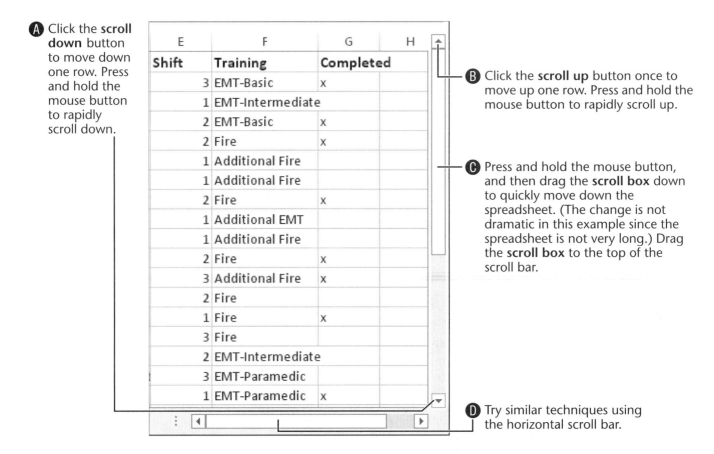

Ⓐ Click the **scroll down** button to move down one row. Press and hold the mouse button to rapidly scroll down.

Ⓑ Click the **scroll up** button once to move up one row. Press and hold the mouse button to rapidly scroll up.

Ⓒ Press and hold the mouse button, and then drag the **scroll box** down to quickly move down the spreadsheet. (The change is not dramatic in this example since the spreadsheet is not very long.) Drag the **scroll box** to the top of the scroll bar.

Ⓓ Try similar techniques using the horizontal scroll bar.

Notice that the active cell does not change position when you scroll through a spreadsheet. Leave the file open.

Navigating with the Keyboard

If your hands are on the keyboard, it may be faster to use keyboard navigation. Excel has keyboard shortcuts for navigating, as shown in the following table. Unlike when scrolling, when you navigate using the keyboard, the active cell moves with you.

KEYBOARD NAVIGATION TECHNIQUES IN EXCEL

Command	Description
Ctrl + Home	Moves to A1
Ctrl + End	Moves to the end of the data in the spreadsheet
Home	Moves to the beginning of the row
Page Down	Moves down one screen
Page Up	Moves up one screen
→ ← ↑ ↓	Moves one cell to the right, left, up, or down

 HANDS-ON 5.3 **Navigate with the Keyboard**

In this exercise, you will use keyboard techniques to move around a spreadsheet.

1. Tap → ← ↓ ↑ on the keyboard a few times to move through the spreadsheet.

2. Press and hold ↓ to produce a repeat action effect.
   All four arrow keys have a repeat action if you hold them down.

3. Press Ctrl + Home to move to cell A1.
   Do you remember the same keystrokes in Word? You're getting twice the benefit from one learned task.

4. Tap Ctrl + End to move to the end of the data in the spreadsheet.

5. Tap Home to move to the beginning of the row.

6. Press Ctrl + Home to move back to A1.

Freezing Panes

You may have a spreadsheet so large that when you scroll down to see the last row of data, the headings at the tops of columns scroll off the screen. It can be difficult to understand the meaning of data if the column headings disappear. The same is true of a wide spreadsheet and row headings. Scrolling to the right could cause the row headings to disappear, again making it difficult to understand what the data represents.

Freezing columns and rows allows you to keep the column and row headings visible while examining data in any part of the spreadsheet—even data that is not close to the headings. The Freeze Panes command options are described in the following table.

FREEZING COLUMNS AND ROWS

Command	Description
Freeze Top Row	As you scroll down the spreadsheet, the top row remains visible. The top row is whatever row appears at the top of the screen when you freeze panes. It may not be row 1.
Freeze First Column	As you scroll to the right, the first column remains visible. The first column is whatever column appears at the left edge of the screen when you freeze panes. It may not be column A.
Freeze Panes	Select a cell and choose the Freeze Panes command to freeze everything above and to the left of the selected cell.
Unfreeze Panes	Unlocks the frozen columns and/or rows.

 HANDS-ON 5.4 **Freeze Panes**

In this exercise, you will freeze rows and columns so they remain static when you scroll in the spreadsheet.

1. Scroll down the spreadsheet until the column headings disappear off the screen.

    Without the column headings, it's difficult to understand the meaning of the data.

2. Press Ctrl + Home to move to cell A1.

    Now you will freeze the first row.

3. Choose **View→Window→Freeze Panes** ▦ then choose **Freeze Top Row**.

    Notice the dark line that appears below row 1, indicating that the freeze action is in effect.

> **!TIP!** The *top row* is the row that happens to appear at the top of the screen at the time you choose Freeze Top Row from the menu; it won't necessarily be row 1.

4. Follow these steps to see the effect of freezing the top row:

 A Scroll down the screen until **row 16** is just below row 1.

◢	A	B	C	D
1	**Last Nam**	**First Name**		**Rank**
16	Alexander	Martin		Firefighter/EMT-Paramedic
17	Mahal	Jasleen		EMT-Basic
18	Wright	Roger		Firefighter/EMT-Intermediat
19	Webster	Alan		EMT-Intermediate
20	Penbrook	Robert		Firefighter/EMT-Paramedic
21	Schultz	Edward		Firefighter/EMT-Intermediat
22	Waldek	John		EMT-Basic
23	Smith	Anthony		Firefighter/EMT-Basic
24	Swan	Edwin		Firefighter
25	Iverson	George		Firefighter/EMT-Basic

B Notice that the column headings in row 1 are still visible, making the meaning of the data easy to understand.

5. Scroll to the top of the spreadsheet.

Now you will freeze the first column.

6. Choose **View→Window→Freeze Panes** then choose **Freeze First Column**.

This unfreezes the first row and freezes the first column. Notice that the dark line is no longer below row 1, and a dark line now appears to the right of column A.

> **!TIP!** The *first column* is the column that happens to appear at the left edge of the screen at the time you choose Freeze First Column; it won't necessarily be column A.

7. Scroll to the right and notice that the first column remains in place.

Now you will unfreeze panes.

8. Choose **View→Window→Freeze Panes** then choose **Unfreeze Panes**.

The dark line to the right of column A disappears.

Freeze Columns and Rows at the Same Time

9. Select **cell D2** to make it the active cell.

10. Choose **View→Window→Freeze Panes** then choose **Freeze Panes**.

Notice the dark horizontal and vertical lines that indicate everything above and to the left of the active cell (D2) is frozen.

11. Follow these steps to scroll in both directions:

Ⓐ Scroll down until **row 5** is just below row 1.

Ⓑ Scroll right until **column F** is next to **column C**.

	A	B	C	F	G	H
1	**Last Nam**	**First Name**		**Training**	**Completed**	
5	Bryan	Henry		EMT-Basic	x	
6	Justin	Oliver		Fire	x	
7	Paulson	Glenn		Additional Fire		
8	Sanchez	Barbara		Additional Fire		
9	Gordon	Maxwell		Fire	x	
10	Frost	Suzanne		Additional EMT		
11	Morgan	Jack		Additional Fire		

12. Choose **View**→**Window**→**Freeze Panes** ⊞ then choose **Unfreeze Panes**.

Entering Data in a Spreadsheet

Now that you're getting comfortable with spreadsheet terminology and navigation, it's time to enter data so you can keep the training roster up to date.

When you start to enter data in a spreadsheet, the Cancel and Enter buttons at the left side of the Formula Bar appear bolder. This indicates that you are *in the process* of entering data.

Cancel ⎯ × ✓ *fx* 123 ⎯ Enter

Completing and Canceling Entries

Entering data is a two-step process. Once you type data in a cell, the next step is to complete the entry. If you suddenly realize that you selected the wrong cell, you may want to cancel the entry. The following table describes the methods you can use to complete and cancel cell entries.

COMPLETING AND CANCELING CELL ENTRIES

Method	Result
Tap Enter	Excel completes the entry; the active cell moves down one row.
Tap Tab	Excel completes the entry; the active cell moves to the right one column.
Tap an arrow key on the keyboard	Excel completes the entry; the active cell moves in the direction of the arrow.
Click the Enter button on the Formula Bar	Excel completes the entry; the active cell remains active.
Click the Cancel button on the Formula Bar	Excel removes any data typed in the cell; the active cell remains active.
Tap Esc	Excel removes any data typed in the cell; the active cell remains active.

 HANDS-ON 5.5 **Enter Data in a Spreadsheet**

In this exercise, you will enter data in a spreadsheet using several data entry techniques as you add a new firefighter to the roster.

1. Follow these steps to enter data in the spreadsheet:

Ⓐ Select **cell A31** and type **Montoya**. Don't tap Enter yet.

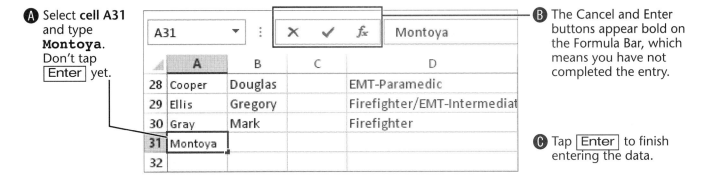

Ⓑ The Cancel and Enter buttons appear bold on the Formula Bar, which means you have not completed the entry.

Ⓒ Tap Enter to finish entering the data.

The Cancel and Enter buttons appear lighter, and the active cell moves down one row.

2. Select **cell A31** again and look at the Formula Bar.

You see that the data you entered appears in the Formula Bar as well as in the cell. Later in this lesson, you will use the Formula Bar to make editing changes.

3. Follow these steps to enter data in cell B31:

A Select **cell B31** and type **Margarita**, but don't tap ⌷Enter⌷.

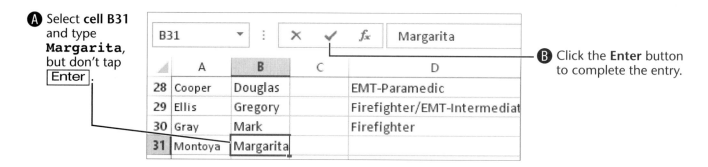

B Click the **Enter** button to complete the entry.

Cell B31 remains the active cell when you use the Enter button.

4. Select **cell D31**, type **Firefighter**, and tap ⌷↓⌷ to complete the entry.

Tapping ⌷↓⌷ has the same effect as tapping ⌷Enter⌷: The active cell moves down one row. Cell D32 is now the active cell.

5. Select **cell E31**, type **3**, and complete the entry by tapping ⌷Tab⌷.

This moves the active cell one column to the right, and cell F31 is now the active cell. You will enter the term *Fire* in cell F31. Because the word *Fire* already appears in column F, Excel will use AutoComplete (similar to Word) to enter the term for you.

6. Type **F** in **cell F31** and watch as Excel autocompletes *Fire*.

7. Tap ⌷Tab⌷ to complete the entry.

> **!TIP!** If you want to type something other than what Excel proposes, just keep typing.

8. Save the file.

QUICK REFERENCE: Deleting, Replacing, and Editing Data

Task	Procedure
Delete an entry	Select the cell and tap ⌷Delete⌷.
Replace an entry	Select the cell, type the new data, and complete the entry.
Edit in the Formula Bar	Select the cell and its data appears in the Formula Bar. Click to place the insertion point in the Formula Bar, and then modify the data.
Use in-cell editing	Double-click the cell to place the insertion point in the cell. Modify the data in the cell.

HANDS-ON 5.6 **Edit Data in a Spreadsheet**

In this exercise, you will use different editing techniques to modify your spreadsheet. You realize that Mark Gray (row 30) did not complete his Additional Fire training yet, so the first thing you will do is delete the "x" in cell G30.

1. Select **cell G30** and tap Delete.

   Oliver Justin's (row 6) last name is incorrect. It should be *Jensen*.

2. Select **cell A6**, type **Jensen**, and tap Enter.

   The correct name replaces the original entry. Next you will correct Oliver's title by adding the word *Firefighter* in front of *EMT-Intermediate*. This time you will edit in the formula bar.

3. Follow these steps to make the correction:

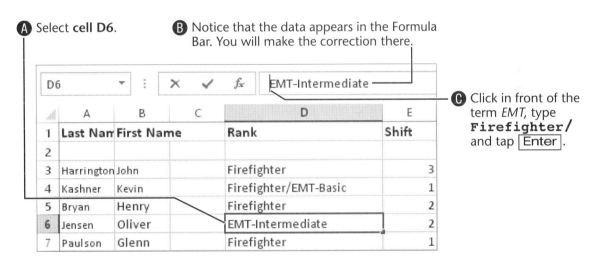

Ⓐ Select **cell D6**.

Ⓑ Notice that the data appears in the Formula Bar. You will make the correction there.

Ⓒ Click in front of the term *EMT*, type **Firefighter/** and tap Enter.

Because Oliver is already a firefighter, he doesn't need Fire training; he needs Additional Fire training. This time you will make the editing change directly in the cell.

4. Double-click **cell F6**.

   This places the insertion point in the cell and causes the mouse pointer to change to an I-beam.

5. If necessary, click in front of *Fire*. Type **Additional**, tap Spacebar, and tap Tab.

   The active cell is now cell G6. Oliver has not completed the Additional Fire training.

6. Tap Delete to remove the "x" from cell G6.

7. Save the file.

Aligning Cell Contents

By default, Excel aligns text to the left edge of cells and numbers to the right edge of cells. You can use the alignment buttons on the Ribbon to modify alignment within cells. They function in a manner similar to the alignment buttons in Word: Align Left, Center, and Align Right.

 HANDS-ON 5.7 **Align Data in Cells**

In this exercise, you will use the alignment buttons to change the alignment of data in your spreadsheet.

1. Select **cell D1**.

2. Choose **Home→Alignment→Align Right** ≡.

3. Choose **Home→Alignment→Center** ≡.

4. Select **cell E1**.

5. Choose **Home→Alignment→Center** ≡.

6. Now center the text in **cell F1**.

7. Save the file.

Working with Cell Ranges

A cell range is a group of adjacent cells. You select (highlight) cell ranges when you want to do something with them, such as formatting, moving, or copying them. You can also use cell ranges in formulas, which you will learn about later in the course.

You identify cell ranges by the cell addresses in the upper-left and lower-right corners of the range. A colon is placed between the two cell addresses, such as A1:C10. This is described as A1 *through* C10.

When you select a range of cells, a white cell appears in the upper-left corner of the range. This is the active cell. If you type data, it will appear in the white cell. The following Quick Reference table describes several techniques for selecting cells.

QUICK REFERENCE: Selecting Cell Ranges

Task	Procedure
Select a range	• Option 1: Select the first cell in the range, press and hold the mouse button, and drag to the last cell.
	• Option 2: Select the first cell in the range, press and hold the Shift key, and click the last cell in the range.
	• Option 3: Click the first cell in the range, hold down the Shift key, and tap the arrow keys to select the range.
Select a column	• Click the column header. For example, to select column A, click directly on the A at the top of the column.
Select a row	• Click the row header. For example, to select row 1, click directly on the 1 at the beginning of the row.
Select the entire spreadsheet	• Click the Select All button (between the row 1 header and the column A header) in the upper-left corner of the spreadsheet.

HANDS-ON 5.8   Select Ranges of Cells

In this exercise, you will use several techniques for selecting cell ranges.

1. Follow these steps to select the range A1:E9.

A Position the mouse pointer in **cell A1**, press and hold the mouse button, and drag down and to the right to **cell E9**.

	A	B	C	D	E
1	Last Nam	First Name		Rank	Shift
2					
3	Harrington	John		Firefighter	3
4	Kashner	Kevin		Firefighter/EMT-Basic	1
5	Bryan	Henry		Firefighter	2
6	Jensen	Oliver		Firefighter/EMT-Intermediat	2
7	Paulson	Glenn		Firefighter	1
8	Sanchez	Barbara		Firefighter/EMT-Paramedic	1
9	Gordon	Maxwell		Paramedic	2

B Release the mouse button, and the range is selected. If you make a mistake, click anywhere in the spreadsheet to deselect the range and try again.

2. Click any cell to deselect the range.

3. Select **cell A1**.

4. Hold down Shift and click **cell E9** to select the range A1:E9.

5. Click any cell to deselect the range.

Select a Range with Arrow Keys

6. Click **cell A1**; then, hold down [Shift] and tap [→] four times to select through **column E**.

7. While holding down [Shift], tap [↓] enough times to highlight through **row 9**.

Notice that the highlighting of the row headers and column headers helps you see which rows and columns you selected.

8. Click any cell to deselect the range.

Next you will select column D. When you select a column, the mouse pointer looks like a down-pointing black arrow.

9. Place the mouse pointer over the column header for **column D** and click.

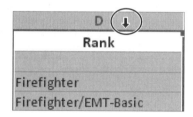

This selects the entire column—all the way down to row 1,048,576.

10. Place the mouse pointer over the row header for **row 1** and click.

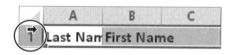

This selects the entire row—all the way over to column 16,384.

11. Place the mouse pointer over the **Select All** button and click.

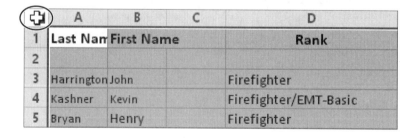

This selects the entire spreadsheet.

12. Press [Ctrl]+[Home] to deselect and make cell A1 the active cell.

Moving and Copying Data

Moving and copying data in a spreadsheet eliminates the need to retype it, thus saving time. When you move data, you remove it from its original position and place it in a new position. When you copy data, the original remains in place while a copy of the data is placed in a new location—so it's in both places.

QUICK REFERENCE: Moving and Copying Data with Cut, Copy, and Paste

Task	Procedure
Move data	• Select the cell(s) you want to move then click the Cut button.
	• Click the destination cell then click the Paste button.
Copy data	• Select the cell(s) you want to copy then click the Copy button.
	• Click the destination cell then click the Paste button.

HANDS-ON 5.9 Move and Copy Data

In this exercise, you will use the Cut, Copy, and Paste buttons to move and copy data.

1. Follow these steps to move data from column F to column I:

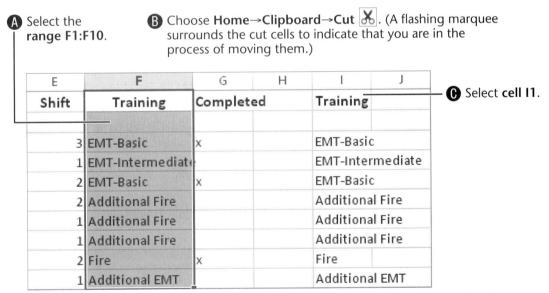

Ⓐ Select the **range F1:F10**.

Ⓑ Choose **Home→Clipboard→Cut**. (A flashing marquee surrounds the cut cells to indicate that you are in the process of moving them.)

Ⓒ Select **cell I1**.

Ⓓ Choose **Home→Clipboard→Paste**. The data moves from the original range to the new range. (At this point there should be no data in F1:F10.)

2. Follow these steps to copy data from column I to column K:

Ⓐ Select the **range I1:I10**.   Ⓑ Choose **Home→Clipboard→Copy** 📋.

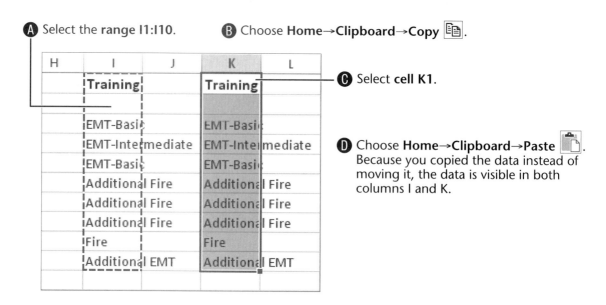

Ⓒ Select **cell K1**.

Ⓓ Choose **Home→Clipboard→Paste** 📋. Because you copied the data instead of moving it, the data is visible in both columns I and K.

The flashing marquee will disappear as you work in the spreadsheet; however, you can make it go away any time by tapping the [Esc] key.

3. If desired, tap [Esc].

4. Save the file.

Sorting Data

Organizing data in a logical sequence often makes the data easier to understand and work with. Sorting information alphabetically or numerically is one of the primary capabilities of a spreadsheet program like Excel. This also means that you can create lists randomly, placing all new entries at the bottom of the list and then asking Excel to sort the list for you.

Kinds of Sorts

The kind of sort Excel offers to perform is based on the type of data in the column by which you want to sort. If you select a cell in an alphabetic column, Excel offers to sort from A to Z or from Z to A. If the column contains numbers, Excel proposes sorting from smallest to largest or from largest to smallest. If the column is populated with dates, Excel will sort from oldest to newest or from newest to oldest.

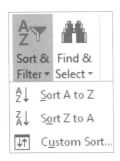

Alphabetic
sort options

Numeric sort options

Date sort options

Structuring an Effective List

There are a few things you should keep in mind when creating a list that you can sort effectively.

- **No blanks:** There can be no blank columns or rows in a list. Blanks can cause serious problems when sorting a list. All data must be adjacent. (It's fine to have blank cells *within* a column/row, but the entire column or row cannot be blank.)

- **Consistent terminology:** This ensures that items that are meant to sort together stay together. For example, if you are a car dealer and you sell SUVs, you shouldn't refer to such vehicles as an *SUV* in one row and as a *sport utility* in another row. Excel does not consider these two terms to be the same.

HANDS-ON 5.10 **Sort Data**

In this exercise, you will perform an alphabetic sort, a numeric sort, and a date sort. You will begin by switching to the Sheet 2 page in your workbook.

1. Click the **Sheet 2** tab at the bottom of the workbook to switch to that spreadsheet.
   Notice that there are no blank columns or rows in this list. That's a prerequisite for a successful sort. Now you'll perform an alphabetic sort.

2. Select any cell in **column A** that is within the list.

3. Choose **Home→Editing→Sort & Filter** ![icon] then choose **Sort A to Z**.
   The list is now in alphabetic order by last name. Now you will perform a date sort.

4. Select any cell in **column C** that is within the list.

5. Choose **Home→Editing→Sort & Filter** then choose **Sort Oldest to Newest**.

   The oldest date appears at the top of the list. Now you will perform a numeric sort.

6. Select any cell in **column E** that is within the list.

7. Choose **Home→Editing→Sort & Filter** then choose **Sort Smallest to Largest**.

   The shifts are now in numeric order starting with the first shift.

8. Save the file.

Working with Columns and Rows

Excel provides the ability to widen and narrow columns and rows, meaning you can adjust them to fit the data you enter in them. Rows automatically adapt to the font size you use. You also have the ability to add and delete columns and rows.

Resizing Columns and Rows

If data is too wide for a column, you can resize it so all of the data fits the column. If the data is narrow, you can narrow the column width.

When you position the mouse pointer on the border between the column headers, it changes to a double-headed arrow.

Press and hold the mouse button and drag to the right/left to widen/narrow the column.

Position the mouse pointer on the border between two rows and drag up/down to narrow/widen the row.

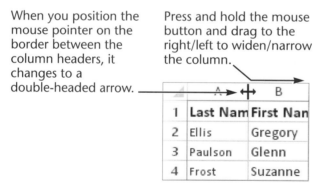

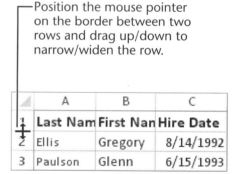

You can also double-click the border between two column headers. This is known as *Best Fit*, and it makes the column wide enough to accommodate the widest entry in the column.

HANDS-ON 5.11 Resize Columns

In this exercise, you will resize columns to accommodate the width of the column headings.

Before You Begin: Make sure Sheet 2 is still active.

1. Position the mouse pointer on the border between **columns A and B.**

   The mouse pointer changes to a double-headed arrow.

	A		B
1	**Last Nam**		**First Nan**
2	Ellis		Gregory
3	Paulson		Glenn
4	Frost		Suzanne

2. Press and hold down the mouse button, and then drag to the right.

3. Release the mouse button when you think *Last Name* is fully visible.

4. If you didn't make the column wide enough, repeat the process until you can see the entire column heading.

5. Position the mouse pointer on the border between **columns B and C.**

   The mouse pointer changes to a double-headed arrow.

6. Press and hold down the mouse button, and then drag to the right to widen the column enough to see the complete column heading.

7. Position the mouse pointer between **columns D and E.**

8. When the pointer changes to a double-headed arrow, double-click and Excel makes the column wide enough for the column data.

9. Use the double-click technique to widen **column G.**

10. Save the file.

Inserting and Deleting Columns and Rows

Once you create a spreadsheet, you may discover that you need to add or remove entire columns or rows. For example, you may need to accommodate a change in the data. You can add or delete a single column or row, or you can add or delete multiple columns or rows at once.

If you select multiple rows or columns before issuing the Insert or Delete command (as described in the following table), the same number of rows or columns that you selected will be inserted or deleted.

QUICK REFERENCE: Inserting and Deleting Columns and Rows

Task	Procedure
Insert rows	• Select the row where you want the new row to appear. • Choose Home→Cells→Insert menu button ▼→Insert Sheet Rows.
Insert columns	• Select the column where you want the new column to appear. • Choose Home→Cells→Insert menu button ▼→Insert Sheet Columns.
Delete rows	• Select the row to delete. • Choose Home→Cells→Delete menu button ▼→Delete Sheet Rows.
Delete columns	• Select the column to delete. • Choose Home→Cells→Delete menu button ▼→Delete Sheet Columns.

 HANDS-ON 5.12 **Insert and Delete Columns and Rows**

In this exercise, you will insert and delete columns and rows in your Training Roster file. A firefighter just transferred from another station in your county. He was hired into the county in 1995. Rather than adding him at the bottom of the list and re-sorting the data, you'll add his record above row 4.

Before You Begin: Make sure Sheet 2 is still active.

1. Position the mouse pointer on the row header for row 4 and then click to select the row.

	A	B	C	D
1	Last Name	First Name	Hire Date	Rank
2	Ellis	Gregory	8/14/1992	Firefighter/EMT-Intermediate
3	Paulson	Glenn	6/15/1993	Firefighter
4	Frost	Suzanne	5/19/1996	Firefighter/EMT-Basic
5	Morgan	Jack	8/1/1996	Firefighter

2. Choose **Home→Cells→Insert** 📇 **menu button** ▼ then choose **Insert Sheet Rows.**

Row 4 is now a blank row.

3. Type the information shown in row 4:

	A	B	C	D	E	F	G
1	Last Name	First Name	Hire Date	Rank	Shift	Training	Completed
2	Ellis	Gregory	8/14/1992	Firefighter/EMT-Intermediate	1	EMT-Paramedic	x
3	Paulson	Glenn	6/15/1993	Firefighter	1	Additional Fire	
4	Malik	Hasan	12/4/1995	Firefighter	1	Additional Fire	

> Some of the firefighters are involved in community outreach programs. As part of the database, the chief wants to track which firefighters are involved in which programs. Now you will add a column for outreach tracking. You will insert the new column between columns D and E.

4. Position the mouse pointer at the top of **column E**.

5. When the mouse pointer changes to a down-pointing arrow, click to select the column.

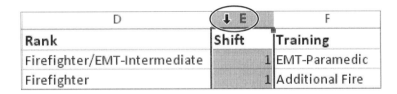

6. Choose **Home→Cells→Insert** 📇 **menu button** ▼ then choose **Insert Sheet Columns**.

> After showing the database to the chief, he said he would rather have the Community Outreach column as the last column. Next you will delete the column you just added.

7. If necessary, position the mouse pointer on the column header for **column E** and click to select the column.

8. Choose **Home→Cells→Delete** 📇 **menu button** ▼ then choose **Delete Sheet Columns**.

> Next you will type the new column heading in H1.

9. Click **cell H1**, type **Community Outreach**, and tap ⌷Enter⌷.

> Now you need to widen the column to accommodate the long heading.

10. Position the mouse pointer on the border between **columns H and I**.

11. When the mouse pointer changes to a double-headed arrow, double-click to widen column H.

12. Save and close the file.

Concepts Review

To check your knowledge of the key concepts introduced in this lesson, complete the Concepts Review quiz here. Or, take the quiz online by going to the student resource center.

True/False Questions

			Page number

1. When you navigate with scroll bars, the active cell does not move. **true** **false** _____

2. When you're in the process of entering data in a spreadsheet, the Cancel and Enter buttons appear bolder on the Formula Bar. **true** **false** _____

3. Only the cells in columns A through Z have addresses. **true** **false** _____

4. Excel's Sort feature allows you to sort numbers but not dates. **true** **false** _____

5. If you want to sort a list, you should not have any blank columns or rows in the list. **true** **false** _____

6. By default, Excel aligns numbers to the left edge of the cell. **true** **false** _____

Multiple Choice Questions

7. What are the three kinds of entries in spreadsheets?

Page number: _____

- **a.** Formulas, text, and numbers
- **b.** Formulas, numbers, and the Ribbon
- **c.** Numbers, text, and cells
- **d.** Numbers, formulas, and columns

8. Use the Freeze Panes feature when _____.

Page number: _____

- **a.** you don't want the data to be modified
- **b.** you want to keep column headings visible while scrolling down
- **c.** you want to select a cell range
- **d.** you want to copy data

9. You may want to add columns or rows to a spreadsheet because _____.

Page number: _____

- **a.** typically there aren't enough cells in an Excel spreadsheet
- **b.** you have to add new columns and rows before you can sort data
- **c.** you must add new columns and rows before you can freeze panes
- **d.** you need to accommodate a change in the data

10. Which of the following *is not* true about cell ranges?

Page number: _____

- **a.** A range of cells is a group of adjacent cells.
- **b.** You must select a range of cells before moving or copying them.
- **c.** When you select a range of cells, the active cell appears in the center of the range.
- **d.** Cell ranges are identified by the cell addresses in the upper-left and lower-right corners of the range.

# Skill Builders

SKILL BUILDER 5.1 **Enter Data and Work with Columns and Rows**

In this exercise, you will review techniques for entering data in a spreadsheet. You are keeping a list of places your friends might like to see when they visit you. Now you are going to add some more places of interest to your list. Remember, entering data is a two-step process. You will also use this opportunity to change the width of a column and to delete a column and a row.

1. Open **sb-Tourist Attractions** from your Lesson 05 folder.

2. Select **cell A17**, type **Blues Festival**, and tap → twice to finish entering the data and move to column C.

   Cell C17 is now the active cell.

3. Type **Fort Mason** and tap → to finish entering the data.

   Cell D17 is now the active cell.

4. Type **September** and tap Enter to finish entering the data.

5. Tap Home to move the active cell to **cell A18**.

6. Type **Grand National Rodeo** and tap → twice to move to **cell C18**.

7. Type **Cow Palace** and tap Tab to enter the data and move to **cell D18**.

8. Type **October–November** in cell D18 and tap Enter to complete the entry.

   The data in column A is flowing into column B. You will adjust column A to accommodate the data.

9. Position the mouse pointer between **columns A and B**.

10. When the mouse pointer changes to a double-headed arrow, drag to the right until the vertical line is to the right of the longest entry; release the mouse button.

Delete a Column and Row

You no longer need column B, and you would also like to delete the blank row 2.

11. Position the mouse pointer on the column header for **column B**.

12. When the mouse pointer changes to a down-pointing arrow, click to select the column.

13. Choose **Home→Cells→Delete** 🔲 **menu button ▾** then choose **Delete Sheet Columns**.

14. Position the mouse pointer on the row header for **row 2**.

15. When the mouse pointer changes to a right-pointing arrow, click to select the row.

16. Choose **Home→Cells→Delete** 🔲 **menu button ▾** then choose **Delete Sheet Rows**.

17. Save and close the file.

SKILL BUILDER 5.2 ## Navigate, Freeze Panes, and Sort Data

In this exercise, you will move around a spreadsheet, freeze panes, and sort data. Your boss asked to see the data represented in a few different ways, and Excel's Freeze Panes and Sort features make preparing data for your boss's review a simple matter.

1. Open **sb-Employee Roster** from your Lesson 05 folder.

2. Click the **scroll down** 🔽 button at the bottom of the scroll bar three times to place row 4 at the top of the spreadsheet.

3. Click the **scroll up** 🔼 button at the top of the scroll bar three times to place row 1 at the top of the window.

4. Click the open part of the **scroll bar** below the scroll box to move down one screen.

5. Press ⟦Ctrl⟧+⟦Home⟧ to move to cell A1.

6. Press ⟦Ctrl⟧+⟦End⟧ to move to the end of the data in the spreadsheet.

7. Tap ⟦Home⟧ to move to the beginning of the row.

8. Tap ⟦Page Up⟧ to move up one screen.

9. Click **cell C2**.

10. Choose **View→Window→Freeze Panes** 🔳 then choose **Freeze Panes**.

11. Scroll down until **row 44** is visible.
    Notice that you can still see the column headings.

12. Scroll to the right until **column F** is next to **column B**.

Unfreeze Panes and Sort Data

13. Choose **View→Window→Freeze Panes** ⊞ then choose **Unfreeze Panes**.

14. Click anywhere in **column I** within the list.

15. Choose **Home→Editing→Sort & Filter** then choose **Sort A to Z**.
    The list is now in alphabetic order by department. Next you will sort by zip code.

16. Click anywhere in **column G** within the list.

17. Choose **Home→Editing→Sort & Filter** then choose **Sort Smallest to Largest**.
    Finally, you will sort by last name.

18. Select **cell A2**.

19. Choose **Home→Editing→Sort & Filter** then choose **Sort A to Z**.

20. Save and close the file.

SKILL BUILDER 5.3 **Select Ranges, Edit, and Copy Data**

In this exercise, you will make editing changes and copy data from one spreadsheet to three other spreadsheets. Your manager asked you to set up an Expenses and Revenues report she can use to track all four regions she is responsible for. The ability to copy data makes this an easy task.

1. Open **sb-Expenses and Revenues by Region** from your Lesson 05 folder.
   Under Expenses, the Rent category should really be Rent/Utilities, so you will make that change first. Then you will add an Advertising category to Expenses.

2. Select **cell B5** and notice the contents of cell B5 in the Formula Bar.

3. Click in the **Formula Bar** following the word *Rent,* type **/Utilities**, and tap Enter.
   Now you'll insert a blank row above row 6 for the Advertising expense category.

4. Position the mouse pointer on the **row 6 header**.

5. When the mouse pointer changes to a right-pointing arrow, click to select the row.

6. Choose **Home→Cells→Insert** menu button ▾ then choose **Insert Sheet Rows**.

7. Select **cell B6**, type **Advertising**, and then tap Enter.

Copy Data from One Spreadsheet to Another

You've already set up spreadsheet tabs for the South, East, and West Regions. Since all four regions have the same expense and revenue items, you can just copy the data from the North Region into the other spreadsheets.

8. Select **cell B2**, and then hold down ⌜Shift⌝ and click **cell D16** to select a range of cells.

9. Choose **Home→Clipboard→Copy** 📋.

10. Click the **South Region tab** to switch to that spreadsheet and then select **cell B2**.

11. Choose **Home→Clipboard→Paste** 📋.

    The data was copied, but notice that the column widths are different from the original. Next you will use the Excel smart tag to keep the column widths the same as the North Region.

12. Follow these steps to keep the original column widths:

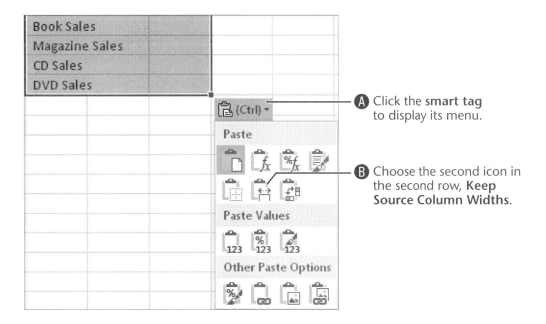

A Click the **smart tag** to display its menu.

B Choose the second icon in the second row, **Keep Source Column Widths.**

    The column widths now match those in the North Region.

13. Click the **North Region tab** and notice that the flashing marquee is still active, indicating that the copied material is still in the Clipboard. You don't have to copy it again.

Copy the Data to the East and West Regions

14. Click the **East Region tab** to switch to that spreadsheet and then select **cell B2**.

15. Choose **Home→Clipboard→Paste** [icon].

16. Click the **smart tag** at the bottom-right corner of the pasted data and choose the second icon in the second row, **Keep Source Column Widths**.

You can now go straight to the West Region tab since the copied information is still in the Clipboard.

17. Click the **West Region tab** and select **cell B2**.

18. Choose **Home→Clipboard→Paste** [icon].

19. Use the **smart tag** to maintain the column widths from the source data.

20. Switch back to the **South Region tab** and correct the region name in **cell D2**.

21. Now correct the East and West Region names.

22. Save and close the file; exit Excel.

Excel – Budgeting with Calculations and Charts

In this lesson, you will perform calculations and create charts in Excel. You will construct your own formulas and use some of Excel's most popular built-in functions. Then you will build eye-catching column and pie charts that summarize data and reveal numeric trends. Picturing your data in charts makes it easy to understand the data at a glance.

LESSON OBJECTIVES

After studying this lesson, you will be able to:

- Work with Excel's mathematical operators
- Build formulas
- Perform calculations using Excel's built-in functions
- Copy formulas and functions
- Create charts to visualize your data

Case Study: Tracking Inventory Expenses

Ken Turner owns a marine supply store on San Francisco Bay. He carefully tracks his inventory budget against actual costs to make sure he keeps his expenses in line.

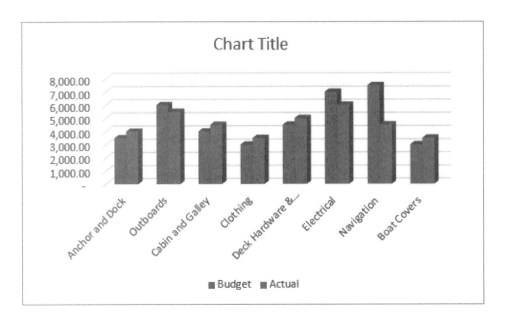

Ken's year-end inventory analysis shows him that his inventory expenses have remained pretty steady throughout the year.

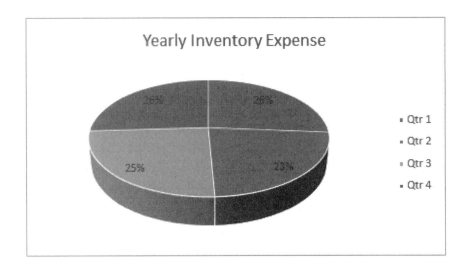

Defining Formulas

Does the word *formula* make you hyperventilate? If the answer is yes, you may be one of those unfortunate people who had an unpleasant introduction to math. Did you know that 2+2 is a formula? Okay, now you can relax.

Just because you use a spreadsheet to perform calculations, it doesn't mean you will suddenly use some strange branch of mathematics. You're going to use the kind of math you have always used; you're just going to do it electronically.

Excel's Mathematical Operators

Mind you, there are a few slight differences in performing calculations electronically versus on paper, but they are not difficult to understand.

You are familiar with the signs used for addition, subtraction, multiplication, and division. If you look around on your keyboard for the division sign you normally use, you won't find it. In Excel, you use the forward slash (/) for the division sign. You use the asterisk (*) for the multiplication sign.

EXCEL'S MATHEMATICAL OPERATORS

Operation	Symbol
Add	+
Subtract	-
Multiply	*
Divide	/

An easy way to remember the operators is to look at the number pad (if your computer has one) on the right side of the keyboard. You can use the keys shown in the following illustration when you create formulas. There are duplicates of these keys on the main part of the keyboard. You can use whichever keys you prefer—or even a combination of them. They all work the same way.

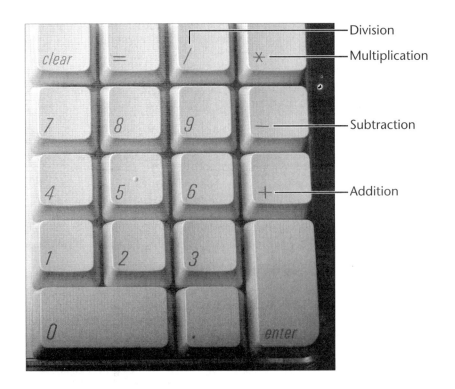

Division — /

Multiplication — *

Subtraction — —

Addition — +

How to Type a Formula

You take a slightly different approach when creating electronic formulas than you do if you are jotting down a formula on a notepad. For example, the placement of the equals (=) sign is different from what you might expect, and in addition to using numbers in formulas, you can use cell addresses, which is typically the preferred method. Both issues will be discussed in more detail.

Where's the Equals Sign?   In Excel, you use the same equals (=) sign you've always used; it's just that you place it at the beginning of the formula rather than at the end.

Instead of typing

    2+2=

You type

    =2+2

Why? When you enter data in a spreadsheet, your computer is watching to see what kind of data it is. If the first thing it sees is a number or an alphabetic character, it assumes that plain old data is coming down the line and it doesn't have to do anything special. If your computer sees an equals (=) sign, it figures, "Hey, this is a formula. I'd better pay attention because I have some work to do. I have to figure out the answer to this formula."

Numbers or Cell Addresses?   You can create formulas using numbers as in the preceding =2+2 example; however, most of the time you should use cell addresses, such as =A1+A2. The reason for this is that if you use numbers in a formula and later decide to change one of those numbers in the spreadsheet, the formula *will not recalculate*. If you use cell addresses, the formula *will recalculate*.

HANDS-ON 6.1   Enter Formulas in a Spreadsheet

In this exercise, you will create formulas in a budget spreadsheet using two techniques. You will begin by calculating the Qtr 1 Budget Total for Other Expenses. Later you will total the entire column, but for now you will just use the four numbers in Other Expenses to keep it simple.

1. If necessary, start **Excel**.

2. Open **Pacific Marine Expense Budget** from your Lesson 06 folder.

3. Take a moment to look over the spreadsheet.

4. Select **cell B17**.
   You always start a formula by selecting the cell that will contain the answer.

    TIP! When you type cell addresses in a formula, you can use either uppercase or lowercase letters. Excel will automatically convert lowercase addresses to uppercase.

5. Type the formula **=B13+B14+B15+B16** then tap ⌷Enter⌷.
   The answer 6,200.00 appears in B17.

6. Select **cell B17** and look at the Formula Bar.
   While the answer appears in cell B17, the formula behind the answer appears in the Formula Bar. This makes it easy to double-check your formulas for accuracy.

   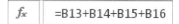

   Now you'll try another formula, but this time you'll get the mouse to help you. You will calculate the Qtr 1 Actual Total for Other Expenses. Again, you are just using four numbers for now to keep it simple.

7. Follow these steps to create a formula using the mouse:

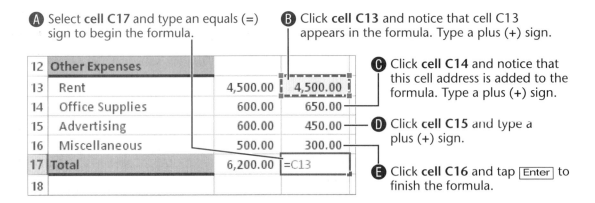

Ⓐ Select **cell C17** and type an equals (=) sign to begin the formula.

Ⓑ Click **cell C13** and notice that cell C13 appears in the formula. Type a plus (+) sign.

Ⓒ Click **cell C14** and notice that this cell address is added to the formula. Type a plus (+) sign.

Ⓓ Click **cell C15** and type a plus (+) sign.

Ⓔ Click **cell C16** and tap ⌷Enter⌷ to finish the formula.

Using the mouse to help you create formulas is easy and reduces the likelihood that you will make a typo.

8. Select **cell C17** and look at the Formula Bar.

The answer appears in cell C17, and the formula appears in the Formula Bar.

Edit a Number That Appears in a Formula

You just discovered that the Actual figure for Miscellaneous expenses should be 400.00 instead of 300.00. Bear in mind that the current answer in cell C17 is 5,900.00.

9. Select **cell C16**, type **400**, and tap ⌷Enter⌷.

Look at the answer in cell C17 (6,000.00). The formula automatically recalculated. Remember, if you use cell addresses in formulas instead of numbers, the formulas recalculate automatically. In the next topic, you'll learn a slicker way to add a column of numbers, so you can delete the formulas you created in this exercise.

10. Click and drag to select **cells B17 and C17**, then tap ⌷Delete⌷.

11. Save the file.

Leave the file open. You will continue to use it throughout the lesson.

Using Built-in Functions

There is another approach you can use to perform calculations. The Excel program has built-in functions that contain formulas that you don't have to write from scratch. This is a real time-saver! The following table shows some of Excel's most popular functions.

COMMON EXCEL FUNCTIONS

Function	Description
=SUM(A1:A100)	Adds the range A1 through A100.
=MAX(A1:A100)	Finds the largest number in the range A1 through A100.
=MIN(A1:A100)	Finds the smallest number in the range A1 through A100.
=AVERAGE(A1:A100)	Finds the average for the range A1 through A100.

How Functions Are Constructed

Functions are built in a specific manner.

- Like all formulas, functions begin with an equals (=) sign.

- Next is the name of the function, such as SUM or AVERAGE.

- After that is a set of parentheses that usually contains one or more arguments. An *argument* is information necessary for the calculation. The range A1:A100 is the argument in each of the examples in the preceding table.

The Sum Button

Probably the most frequently used function is SUM; therefore, Excel provides the convenient Sum button on the Ribbon to automatically calculate sums for you.

 NOTE! Depending on your screen's resolution, this button may be labeled AutoSum. The ToolTip labels the button as Sum. The button will be described as the Sum button in this course.

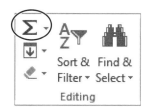

What Do the Pound Signs Mean?

When you have alphabetic or alphanumeric data that is too wide for a cell, if there is data to the right of that cell, Excel visually chops off the text. It's pretty obvious that the column is too narrow, and you can widen it. When it comes to the answers to formulas, if Excel chopped off part of the number, you may not realize it—and you might assume that what you see is correct. To prevent that, Excel places pound signs in the cell as a warning that the column needs to be widened to see the entire number.

4,500.00
650.00
450.00
400.00
########

HANDS-ON 6.2 Use the SUM Function

In this exercise, you will use the SUM function to add a series of numbers in the Budget and Actual columns for the first quarter. First, you will *manually* type the function; then you will use the Sum button to *automatically* enter the function. Finally, you will create a subtraction formula from scratch.

1. Select **cell B17**, type the function **=SUM(B4:B16)**, and tap Enter to complete the function.

2. Ignore the prompts that pop up when you type functions. You will not use them in this lesson.

   Remember, in the last exercise you only added the four numbers in rows 13 through 16 to avoid typing lots of cell addresses. With the convenient SUM function, you can easily indicate a *range* of cell addresses rather than typing each cell address. This method is particularly convenient when adding a long row or column of numbers. Now you will use the Sum button to automatically create a formula.

3. Select **cell C17**.

4. Choose **Home→Editing→Sum** Σ.

   The Sum feature adds a flashing marquee around cells C13 through C16. Sum only went up to C13 because of the blank cell in C12. This isn't correct; you want to add the entire column, C4:C16. No problem; you can easily override Sum's decision.

5. Follow these steps to total the entire column:

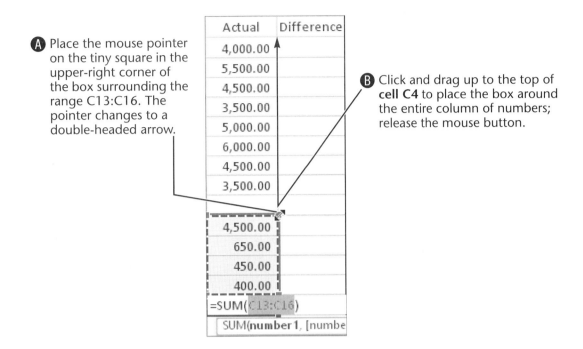

A Place the mouse pointer on the tiny square in the upper-right corner of the box surrounding the range C13:C16. The pointer changes to a double-headed arrow.

B Click and drag up to the top of **cell C4** to place the box around the entire column of numbers; release the mouse button.

The formula is now =SUM(C4:C16).

6. Tap Enter to complete the formula.

Excel places pound signs in the cell. That's because the answer to the formula is too wide to fit in the cell.

7. Position the mouse pointer on the border between the column headers for **columns C and D**. When the mouse pointer changes to a double-headed arrow, double-click to adjust the column width.

!NOTE! Continue to use this technique when you need to widen columns throughout this lesson.

Here's another technique to make sure Sum adds the numbers you want it to.

8. Click and drag to select the **range E4:E17**.

You're selecting the column of numbers you want to add plus a blank cell at the bottom of the column. This is telling Excel to place the answer in the blank cell.

9. Choose **Home→Editing→Sum Σ**.

Excel places the answer in cell E17.

10. Click **cell E17** and check out the formula in the Formula Bar.

11. Widen **column E**.

12. Use the same technique to add the numbers in **column F**; widen the column.
   You can also use that technique with multiple columns at the same time.

13. Select the **range H4:I17**.

14. Choose **Home→Editing→Sum** Σ.
   Excel placed answers in cells H17 and I17.

15. Check out the formulas in the Formula Bar; widen the columns.

16. Use the same technique to add the numbers in **columns K and L** at the same time; widen the columns.

Enter a Subtraction Formula

There is no built-in function for a simple subtraction problem, so you need to create this formula yourself—but you can get the mouse to give you a hand (paw).

17. Select **cell D4** and type an equals (=) sign.

18. Click **cell B4** and type a minus (−) sign.

19. Click **cell C4**, and then tap ⌑Enter⌑ to finish the formula.

20. Click **cell D4** and check the Formula Bar.
   The Actual Anchor and Dock inventory expense was 500.00 over budget; therefore, the answer is in parentheses to indicate a negative number.

   You don't have to retype this formula for all the numbers in columns B and C. Later you will learn to copy formulas—another big time-saver in Excel.

21. Select **cell G4** and type an equals (=) sign.

22. Click **cell E4** and type a minus (−) sign.

23. Click **cell F4** and then tap ⌑Enter⌑ to finish the formula.

24. Use the same technique to enter subtraction formulas in **cells J4 and M4**.
   The parentheses in the answers indicate that you were over budget for Anchor and Dock supplies for the first three quarters and under budget for the fourth quarter.

25. Save the file.

Calculating with AVERAGE, MAX, and MIN

The AVERAGE function calculates the average of a range of cells. The MAX function finds the largest number in a range, while MIN determines the smallest number in a range.

 HANDS-ON 6.3 Use AVERAGE, MAX, and MIN

In this exercise, you will use the AVERAGE, MAX, and MIN functions to quickly analyze inventory data in your workbook.

1. Click the **Inventory Analysis** tab at the bottom of the workbook to switch to that spreadsheet.

    First you will calculate the average of the four quarters. Again, you will get the mouse to help you.

2. Select **cell F2** and type **=AVERAGE(** but don't type the cell addresses.

3. Click and drag to select the **range B2:E2**.

    Notice that the range addresses automatically appear in the formula. You don't have to type the right parenthesis; Excel will do that for you.

4. Tap Enter.

5. Select **cell F2** and check out the Formula Bar.

    You can see that Excel put the right parenthesis in the formula for you.

6. Select **cell G2** and type **=MAX(** but don't type the cell addresses.

7. Click and drag to select the **range B2:E2** and then tap Tab to finish the function and make cell H2 active.

8. Type **=MIN(** in cell H2.

9. Click and drag to select the **range B2:E2** and tap Enter.

    Remember, you're going to learn to copy formulas soon, so you don't have to create these formulas for every row.

10. Save the file.

Copying Formulas and Functions

You can copy formulas and functions because Excel automatically changes cell addresses in a copied formula *relative to* where it is copied. For example, if the =SUM(A1:A100) function is copied one column to the right (column B), the function changes to =SUM(B1:B100).

Here's another example: If you copy the function =SUM(B9:H9) down one row (row 10), the function changes to =SUM(B10:H10). This is known as *relative referencing*, and it's one of the great powers of electronic spreadsheets. Without relative referencing, you would have to create formulas and functions one at a time.

You can use the same Copy button to copy formulas that you use to copy other types of data.

 HANDS-ON 6.4 **Copy Functions and Formulas**

In this exercise, you will copy functions and formulas in both spreadsheets in your workbook. You will start with the =AVERAGE function in F2.

Before You Begin: Make sure the Inventory Analysis worksheet is still active.

1. Select **cell F2**.

2. Choose **Home→Clipboard→Copy** 📋.
   Excel places a flashing marquee around the cell you are copying.

3. Select the **range F3:F9**.

4. Choose **Home→Clipboard→Paste** 📋.

5. Tap Esc to turn off the marquee.

6. Click **cell F2** and examine the formula; click **cell F3** and examine the formula.
   Notice that the range of cells inside the parentheses changed from B2:E2 to B3:E3. Excel changed the cell addresses *relative to* where the formula was copied. Now you will copy the MAX and MIN functions.

7. Select **cell G2**.

8. Choose **Home→Clipboard→Copy** 📋 and then select the **range G3:G9**.

9. Choose **Home→Clipboard→Paste** 📋.

10. Select **cell H2**; copy the function there and paste it into **H3:H9**.
    Now you will calculate the inventory totals for all four quarters at once.

11. Select the **range B2:E10**.

12. Choose **Home→Editing→Sum** Σ.
    Excel places the total for each column in row 10.

Copy the Formulas in the Difference Columns

13. Click the **Expense Budget** tab at the bottom of the workbook to switch to that spreadsheet.

14. Select **cell D4**.

15. Choose **Home→Clipboard→Copy** 📋 and then select the **range D5:D16**.

Note that you won't copy the formula to D17 since row 17 is labeled as a Total row. You are not totaling the Difference column; you are copying the subtraction formula.

16. Choose **Home→Clipboard→Paste** 📋.

Take a moment to examine a couple of copied formulas and notice that the cell addresses changed in a relative fashion.

Row 12 should be blank, so now you will delete the formula in cell D12.

17. Select **cell D12** and tap ⬚Delete.

18. Use the same technique to copy the Difference formulas in **columns G, J, and M**; then, delete **cells G12, J12, and M12**.

19. Save the file.

Using Charts to Visualize Data

Excel's charting features make charting data easy, and the results are stunning. Depicting your data with charts allows you to easily see trends and make comparisons in your data.

Excel offers a variety of chart types. Two of the most common are column and pie charts. Column charts compare categories of data using vertical columns. Each column represents values from a data series in the spreadsheet. Pie charts are round (like pies) and are used for comparing parts (slices) of the whole (pie).

Which Cells Do I Select?

To create a chart, you start by selecting the data you want to represent. Knowing which cells to select prior to creating the chart is important.

Column Charts Column charts compare values across categories. For a column chart, you select the data but typically not a total row or total column. The following data selection allows you to compare the various Inventory categories to each other by quarter, but it does not include the totals from row 10.

	A	B	C	D	E	F
1	Actual Inventory Expense	Qtr 1	Qtr 2	Qtr 3	Qtr 4	Avg of Qtrs
2	Anchor and Dock	4,000.00	3,500.00	3,000.00	2,500.00	3,250.00
3	Outboards	5,500.00	3,000.00	5,000.00	7,000.00	5,125.00
4	Cabin and Galley	4,500.00	4,500.00	4,000.00	4,500.00	4,375.00
5	Clothing	3,500.00	1,500.00	3,500.00	3,000.00	2,875.00
6	Deck Hardware & Fasteners	5,000.00	4,000.00	6,000.00	3,750.00	4,687.50
7	Electrical	6,000.00	6,750.00	4,500.00	6,500.00	5,937.50
8	Navigation	4,500.00	4,500.00	5,500.00	4,000.00	4,625.00
9	Boat Covers	3,500.00	4,000.00	3,000.00	4,500.00	3,750.00
10	Total	36,500.00	31,750.00	34,500.00	35,750.00	

The following chart was created from the data selected in the previous illustration. It compares the Inventory categories across four quarters. For example, you can see that Qtr 1 was the highest inventory cost for Anchor and Dock supplies, while Qtr 4 was the highest inventory cost for Outboards.

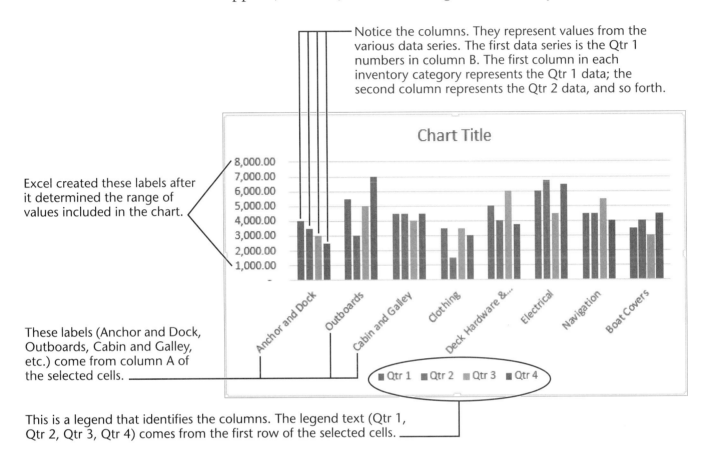

Notice the columns. They represent values from the various data series. The first data series is the Qtr 1 numbers in column B. The first column in each inventory category represents the Qtr 1 data; the second column represents the Qtr 2 data, and so forth.

Excel created these labels after it determined the range of values included in the chart.

These labels (Anchor and Dock, Outboards, Cabin and Galley, etc.) come from column A of the selected cells.

This is a legend that identifies the columns. The legend text (Qtr 1, Qtr 2, Qtr 3, Qtr 4) comes from the first row of the selected cells.

Pie Charts   Pie charts compare pieces of the whole. You typically select two sets of data: the values to be represented by the slices of the pie (totals in row 10 in the following example) and the legend data to identify the slices (row 1 in the following example).

TIP!   To select nonadjacent ranges of cells, select the first range, and then press and hold Ctrl while dragging over additional ranges.

	A	B	C	D	E	
1	Actual Inventory Expense	Qtr 1	Qtr 2	Qtr 3	Qtr 4	Legend labels
2	Anchor and Dock	4,000.00	3,500.00	3,000.00	2,500.00	
3	Outboards	5,500.00	3,000.00	5,000.00	7,000.00	
4	Cabin and Galley	4,500.00	4,500.00	4,000.00	4,500.00	
5	Clothing	3,500.00	1,500.00	3,500.00	3,000.00	
6	Deck Hardware & Fasteners	5,000.00	4,000.00	6,000.00	3,750.00	
7	Electrical	6,000.00	6,750.00	4,500.00	6,500.00	
8	Navigation	4,500.00	4,500.00	5,500.00	4,000.00	
9	Boat Covers	3,500.00	4,000.00	3,000.00	4,500.00	Values
10	Total	36,500.00	31,750.00	34,500.00	35,750.00	represented by the slices of the pie
11						

This chart was created from the data selected in the previous illustration. The slices compare the total inventory expense for each of the four quarters to each other. The inventory expenses for each quarter are almost equal.

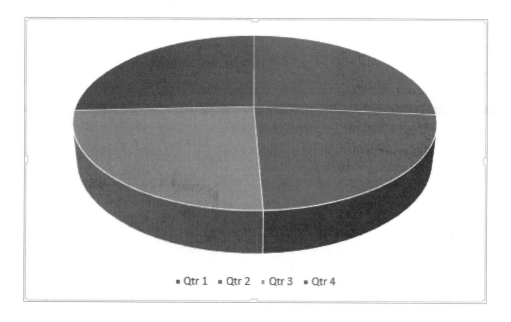

■ Qtr 1 ■ Qtr 2 ■ Qtr 3 ■ Qtr 4

Embedded Charts Compared to Chart Sheets

A chart can either be embedded with the data in the spreadsheet or appear on a separate sheet in the workbook. An embedded chart provides the benefit of making it easy to compare the data in the spreadsheet with the columns or slices in the chart. On the other hand, you may prefer to examine trends and comparisons without focusing on numeric detail. A separate chart sheet works well for that. A chart sheet also makes it easy to print only the chart without the surrounding data.

HANDS-ON 6.5 **Visualize Your Data with Charts**

In this exercise, you will create two charts, a column chart and a pie chart, and you will create both embedded charts and a chart sheet.

1. Click the **Inventory Analysis** tab to switch to that spreadsheet.

2. Select the **range A1:E9**.

3. Choose **Insert→Charts→Insert Column Chart** 📊.

   The column chart gallery opens, from which you can choose various types of column charts.

4. Choose the first chart type in the 2-D Column category.

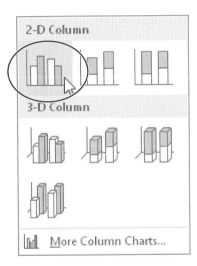

The chart appears in the spreadsheet. It's covering some of the data, but that's okay for now. The border surrounding the chart indicates that it's selected. The chart must be selected if you want to make changes to it. Notice the contextual Chart Tools tabs (Design and Format) that appear on the Ribbon when the chart is selected.

5. Click in the spreadsheet to deselect the chart.

   The chart's surrounding border disappears, as well as the Chart Tools tabs.

6. Click the outer edge of the chart and the border reappears.

   Now you will move the embedded chart to its own chart sheet.

7. Choose **Chart Tools→Design→Location→Move Chart** 📊.

   The Move Chart dialog box appears. Here you can specify to move the chart to a New Sheet. The *Object In* option in the dialog box refers to embedding a chart as an object in the spreadsheet, which is the option currently in effect.

8. Choose **New Sheet** and then click **OK**.

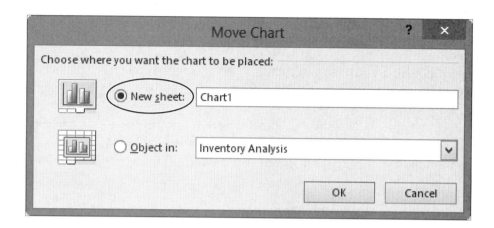

The chart now has its own sheet in the workbook. Notice the Chart 1 tab at the bottom of the workbook.

9. Click the **Inventory Analysis tab** to return to the inventory data.

Notice that the embedded chart no longer appears in the spreadsheet.

Create a Pie Chart

Now you will select data from the Total row to be represented by the pie slices. You will also select the column headings, which will appear in the legend. Remember that you can select multiple nonadjacent ranges by holding down Ctrl when selecting the second and subsequent ranges.

10. Select the **range B1:E1**.

11. Hold down Ctrl and select the **range B10:E10**; release the Ctrl key.

The numbers in the range B10:E10 will determine the size of the slices. The entries in the range B1:E1 will become the entries in the legend, describing the meanings of the slices.

12. Choose **Insert→Charts→Insert Pie or Doughnut Chart** .

The pie chart gallery appears.

13. Choose the chart type in the **3-D Pie category**.

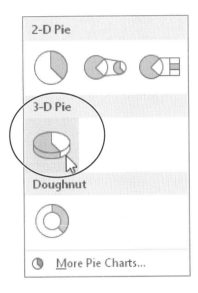

The pie chart now appears, embedded in the spreadsheet.

14. Save the file.

Moving and Resizing an Embedded Chart You can move an embedded chart within a spreadsheet by dragging it with the mouse pointer when the pointer looks like a four-headed arrow. You can resize the chart when the mouse pointer looks like a double-headed arrow.

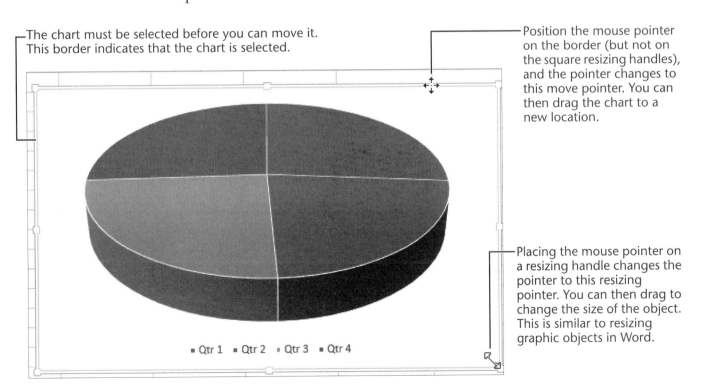

The chart must be selected before you can move it. This border indicates that the chart is selected.

Position the mouse pointer on the border (but not on the square resizing handles), and the pointer changes to this move pointer. You can then drag the chart to a new location.

Placing the mouse pointer on a resizing handle changes the pointer to this resizing pointer. You can then drag to change the size of the object. This is similar to resizing graphic objects in Word.

HANDS-ON 6.6 **Move and Resize an Embedded Chart**

In this exercise, you will move the embedded pie chart below the spreadsheet data. Then you will resize it.

1. If necessary, click the outer edge of the chart to select it.

2. Follow these steps to move the chart:

Ⓐ Place the mouse pointer on the chart border (but not on a resizing handle). Notice that the mouse pointer looks like a four-headed arrow.

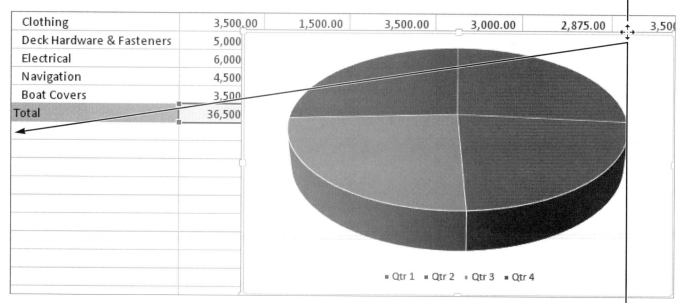

Clothing	3,500.00	1,500.00	3,500.00	3,000.00	2,875.00	3,500
Deck Hardware & Fasteners	5,000
Electrical	6,000
Navigation	4,500
Boat Covers	3,500
Total	36,500

■ Qtr 1 ■ Qtr 2 ■ Qtr 3 ■ Qtr 4

Ⓑ Press and hold down the mouse button, and drag the chart to position its upper-left corner as shown in column A and below the Total row. Release the mouse button.

Now you'll resize the chart.

3. If necessary, scroll down until the bottom-right corner of the chart border is visible.

4. Place the mouse pointer on the bottom-right resizing handle and notice that the pointer changes to a two-headed arrow.

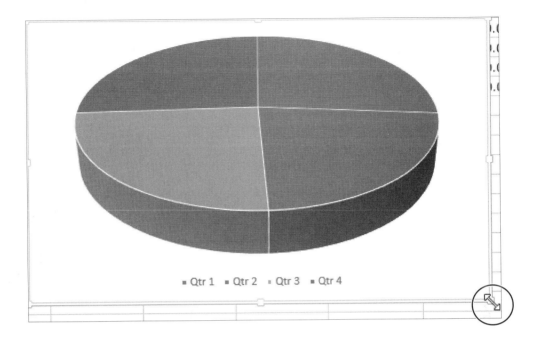

5. Drag up and to the left about a half inch to make the chart smaller.

6. Click in the spreadsheet to deselect the chart.

7. Save the file.

Design Tools

When you select a chart, two new Chart Tools tabs appear on the Ribbon: Design and Format. In this lesson, you will spend some time working with the Design tab. It contains some appealing features for modifying your chart.

Switch Row/Column Data   Switching the row and column data in a column chart provides an interesting change of perspective in analyzing your data. This illustration displays the quarters as the legend and the inventory categories as the labels for the columns in the chart.

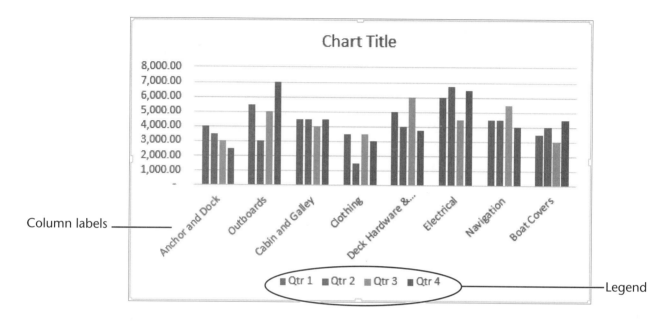

Switching the row and column data provides this new perspective. Notice that the quarters now appear as column labels and the categories make up the legend.

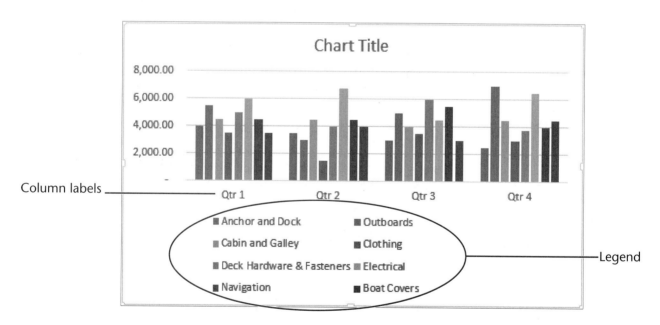

Chart Layouts   The Chart Layouts group on the Design tab provides various methods for labeling pieces of a chart, including numeric values and percentages of the whole.

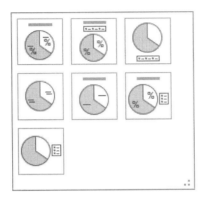

In the following example, the chosen layout displays the slices of the pie as percentages of the whole. Excel added a Chart Title object, which you can modify with your own words.

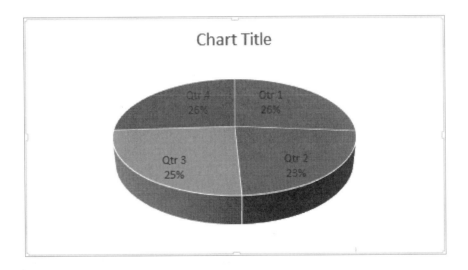

Chart Styles   The Chart Styles gallery offers exciting design and color combinations you can apply to your charts.

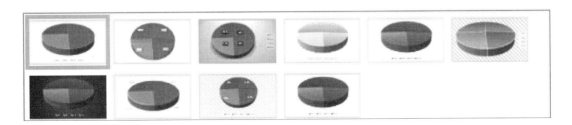

This dramatic change to the chart style was accomplished with a simple click of the mouse.

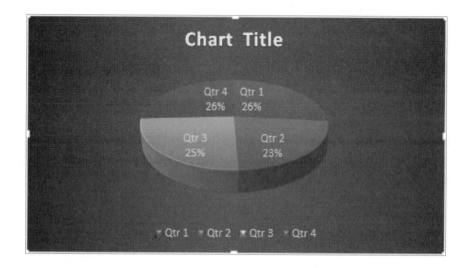

 HANDS-ON 6.7 **Modify the Chart Design**

In this exercise, you will modify the design of charts by switching row and column data, applying a new layout, and applying a new chart style.

1. Click the **Chart 1** tab at the bottom of the workbook to display the column chart.

   Observe the labels at the bottom of the chart and the legend below that. They will switch places when you switch the row and column data.

2. Click the border of the chart to select it.

3. Choose **Chart Tools→Design→Data→Switch Row/Column** 📊.

   Observe the changes to the chart. The quarters appear at the bottom of the columns and the legend is below that. Now you will change a chart layout.

4. Click the **Inventory Analysis** tab at the bottom of the workbook to return to the pie chart.

5. If necessary, click the outer edge of the chart to select it.

6. Choose **Chart Tools→Design→Chart Layouts→Quick Layout** 📊 to display various layouts.

7. Choose **Layout 6**.

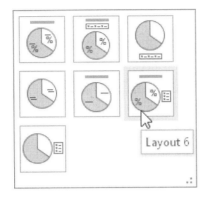

8. Follow these steps to observe the changes to the chart:

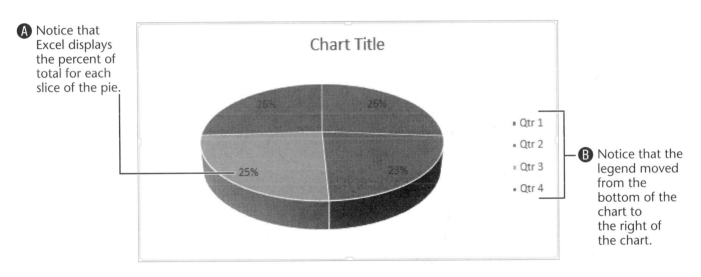

Ⓐ Notice that Excel displays the percent of total for each slice of the pie.

Ⓑ Notice that the legend moved from the bottom of the chart to the right of the chart.

Now you will type a new chart title.

9. Click the **Chart Title** object to select it.

10. Type **Yearly Inventory Expense** as the new chart title and tap Enter.

Change the Chart Style

11. Choose **Chart Tools→Design→Chart Styles**.

12. Click the **More** button at the right edge of the Chart Styles gallery to display the entire gallery.

Chart Styles

13. Choose **Style** 3. Use ToolTips to assist you if necessary.

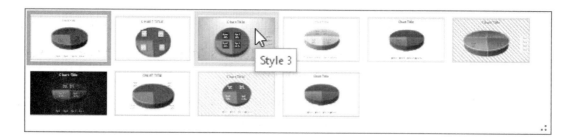

The chart now has a dramatic new look.

14. Save and close the file.

Concepts Review

To check your knowledge of the key concepts introduced in this lesson, complete the Concepts Review quiz here. Or, take the quiz online by going to the student resource center.

True/False Questions

			Page number

1. Using charts allows you to easily see trends and make comparisons about your data.   **true**   **false**   _____

2. All formulas and functions begin with an equals (=) sign.   **true**   **false**   _____

3. The multiplication symbol in Excel is "x."   **true**   **false**   _____

4. Excel automatically changes the cell addresses in a copied formula relative to where it's copied.   **true**   **false**   _____

5. If you want formulas to recalculate when a number changes, use numbers and not cell addresses.   **true**   **false**   _____

6. An Excel chart can be embedded in a spreadsheet or appear on a separate chart sheet.   **true**   **false**   _____

Multiple Choice Questions

7. Which of the following *is not* one of Excel's built-in functions?

Page number: _____

a. MAX

b. SUBTRACT

c. AVERAGE

d. SUM

8. Which of the following is a mathematical operator in Excel?

Page number: _____

a. ?

b. /

c. &

d. #

9. Which of the following *is not* an Excel chart type?

Page number: _____

a. Pie

b. Line

c. Column

d. Medical

10. Why do Excel formulas begin with an equals sign?

Page number: _____

a. It's easier to type the equals sign at the beginning of the formula than at the end.

b. Excel uses a different branch of mathematics than you learned in school.

c. It indicates to Excel that the data is a formula.

d. It's the only key on the keyboard not reserved for other purposes.

Skill Builders

SKILL BUILDER 6.1 **Track the Men's Championship Golf Tournament**

In this exercise, you will use some of Excel's built-in functions. You are in charge of keeping track of the golf scores for the Men's Championship. It's the perfect opportunity for you to get more experience with entering and copying functions.

1. Open **sb-Golf Scores** from your Lesson 06 folder.

2. Enter the data as shown for **rows 6–11**.

	A	B	C	D	E	F	G	H	I
1	Golf Week Men's Championship								
2									
3									
4									
5	Name	Day 1	Day 2	Day 3	Day 4	Tournament Total	Tournament Avg	Tournament Max	Tournament Min
6	Mukesh Patel	70	66	67	68				
7	Roger Kashner	72	68	69	71				
8	Moses LeVan	71	70	73	73				
9	Jose Menendez	70	69	76	75				
10	Albert Schultz	73	71	71	76				
11	Arnold Alvarez	69	75	75	72				

Now you'll use the SUM function to calculate the tournament total for each player.

3. Select **cell F6**.

4. Choose **Home→Editing→Sum** Σ.

Excel places a marquee around Mukesh Patel's scores for the four days of the tournament.

5. Click the **Enter** ✔ button on the Formula Bar to finish entering the function.

Now you will copy the function for the rest of the players. Cell F6 should still be active.

6. Choose **Home→Clipboard→Copy** 📋 and then select the **range F7:F11**.

7. Choose **Home→Clipboard→Paste** 📋.

8. Tap Esc to remove the flashing marquee.

Mukesh Patel is our winner! He has the lowest score for the four-day tournament. Next you will calculate Mukesh's average score.

Use the AVERAGE, MAX, and MIN Functions

9. Select **cell G6** and type **=AVERAGE(** .

10. Select the **range B6:E6** and tap ⌷Tab⌷ to complete the formula.
    Now you will calculate Mukesh's maximum and minimum scores.

11. With **cell H6** the active cell, type **=MAX(** .

12. Select the **range B6:E6** and tap ⌷Tab⌷ to finish entering the formula.

13. With **cell I6** the active cell, type **=MIN(** .

14. Select the **range B6:E6** and tap ⌷Enter⌷.
    Now you will copy all three functions for the rest of the players at the same time.

15. Select the **range G6:I6**.

16. Choose **Home→Clipboard→Copy** 📋 and then select the **range G7:I11**.

17. Choose **Home→Clipboard→Paste** 📋.
    Now you see the average, maximum, and minimum scores for all of the players.

18. Tap ⌷Esc⌷ to turn off the marquee.

19. Save and close the file.

SKILL BUILDER 6.2 ## Calculate Nutrients and Chart the Data

Your doctor has been complaining about your fondness for junk food. She wants you to have more calcium, protein, and fiber (and less cholesterol and saturated fats) in your diet. In this exercise, you will examine the nutritional value of various foods and use a chart to depict the data.

1. Open **sb-Counting Nutrients** from the Lesson 06 folder.

   You will use the MAX and MIN functions to determine which foods are the highest and lowest in various nutrient categories.

2. Select **cell C12** and type **=MAX(** .

3. Select the **range C5:C10** and tap ⌷Enter⌷.
   Broccoli wins in the Calcium category.

4. Type **=MIN(** in **cell C13**.

5. Select the **range C5:C10** and tap ⌷Enter⌷.
   Now you will copy the formulas.

6. Select the **range C12:C13**.

7. Choose **Home→Clipboard→Copy** 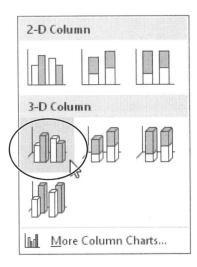 and then select the **range D12:G13**.

8. Choose **Home→Clipboard→Paste** .

9. Tap Esc to turn off the marquee.

   Now you see the maximum and minimum values for each nutrient category.

Chart the Nutrients

10. Select the **range B4:G10**.

11. Choose **Insert→Charts→Insert Column Chart** .

12. Choose the first chart type in the **3-D category**.

   Notice which of the foods are high and low in the various nutrient categories.

13. Drag the chart below the data and position it where you think it looks best.

14. Click in the spreadsheet to deselect the chart.

15. Save and close the file.

Create a Household Budget

In this exercise, you will use your Excel skills to add formulas to your household budget. First you will compute the total monthly income and then you will find the total for all expense categories. Finally, you will subtract total expenses from total income to determine if you are over or under budget for the month.

1. Open **sb-Household Budget** from the Lesson 06 folder.

2. Select **cell C8**.

3. Choose **Home→Editing→Sum** Σ and then tap ⌈Enter⌉ to complete the formula.

   There's your total monthly income. Let's hope it's enough to cover the expenses.

4. Select **cell C14**.

5. Choose **Home→Editing→Sum** Σ and then tap ⌈Enter⌉ to complete the formula.

6. Use the **Sum** Σ button to enter the totals for the remaining expense categories in **cells C22, C30, and C35**.

   Next you will compute Total Expenses for January.

Create Formulas from Scratch

7. Select **cell C38** and use the mouse to help you create this formula: **=C14+C22+C30+C35**

8. Tap ⌈Enter⌉ to complete the formula.

   Now you will determine whether you are under or over budget.

9. With **cell C39** the active cell, enter the formula **=C8–C38** and tap ⌈Enter⌉.

   Congratulations! You are well under budget for the month.

10. Save and close the file.

Track Your Stocks

In this exercise, you will track a stock you are thinking about investing in. You want to examine its performance over time to see how it's doing.

1. Open **sb-Stock Tracker** from your Lesson 06 folder.

   Seven weeks ago the XYZ stock closed at 36. You want to see how you would have fared if you had purchased 100 shares of the stock. First you will calculate the total purchase price by multiplying the original price per share by the number of shares owned.

2. Select **cell E4** and type the formula **=C4*D4**.

3. Click the **Enter** ✔ button on the Formula Bar.

4. Copy the formula in **cell E4** down through **cell E9**.

5. Use this information to enter Week End Prices in the **range B4:B9**:

Week 1	38
Week 2	39
Week 3	42
Week 4	35
Week 5	37
Week 6	39

   Now you will calculate the value for each week-ending period by multiplying the week-end price by the number of shares owned.

6. Select **cell F4** and type the formula **=B4*D4**.

7. Click the **Enter** ✔ button to complete the formula.

8. Copy the formula in **cell F4** down through **cell F9**.

   And now you will compute the total earnings for each week-ending period by subtracting the total purchase price from the current value.

9. Click **cell G4**, type the formula **=F4–E4**, and click **Enter** ✔.

10. Copy the formula in **cell G4** down through **cell G9**.

11. Tap [Esc] to turn off the marquee.

Chart Your Data

12. Select the **range F3:G9.**

13. Choose **Insert→Charts→Insert Column Chart** 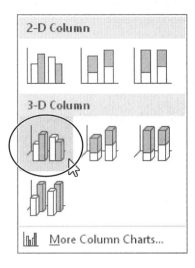.

14. Choose the first chart type in the **3-D Column category.**

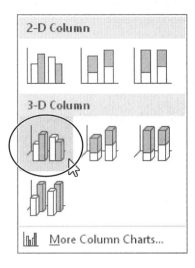

15. Drag the chart below the data.

16. Click in the spreadsheet to deselect the chart.

17. Save and close the file.

Graph a Giraffe

In this exercise, you will create a giraffe graph. You are pursuing a degree in Animal Care and Technology, and you think it would be interesting to track the heights of giraffes in the area zoos. Your local zookeeper has provided you with the height of each giraffe.

1. Open **sb-Giraffe Heights** from the Lesson 06 folder.

   There are nine giraffes at the zoo: two adult males, three adult females, two yearlings, and two babies.

2. Select the **range A3:D6**.

3. Choose **Insert→Charts→Insert Column Chart** .

4. Choose the first chart type in the **3-D Column category**.

   Now you will move the chart to its own sheet.

5. Make sure the chart is selected.

6. Choose **Chart Tools→Design→Location→Move Chart** .

7. Choose the **New Sheet** option in the Move Chart dialog box and click **OK**.

   The chart now appears on its own page in the workbook.

8. Save and close the file; exit Excel.

LESSON 7

PowerPoint – Creating Powerful Presentations

In this lesson, you will learn the basics of PowerPoint 2013. You will create a PowerPoint presentation, apply a variety of layouts and design themes to your slides, explore several ways to view your slides, and add interest to your presentation with clip art, animations, and transitions.

LESSON OBJECTIVES

After studying this lesson, you will be able to:

- Identify key parts of the PowerPoint window
- Navigate through a presentation
- Work with design themes and slide layouts
- Explore the different PowerPoint views
- Add clip art, animations, and transitions

Case Study: Creating an Email Presentation

Alec Harkins is a time management expert. He has been invited to give a presentation on efficient use of email at Central College Career Day next month. Knowing the impact of email, he wants to create a presentation that will give his audience the tools they need to get their email under control. Alec's dynamic speaking abilities, coupled with PowerPoint's robust presentation features, are sure to win over the audience.

Alec adds interest to his presentation with clip art.

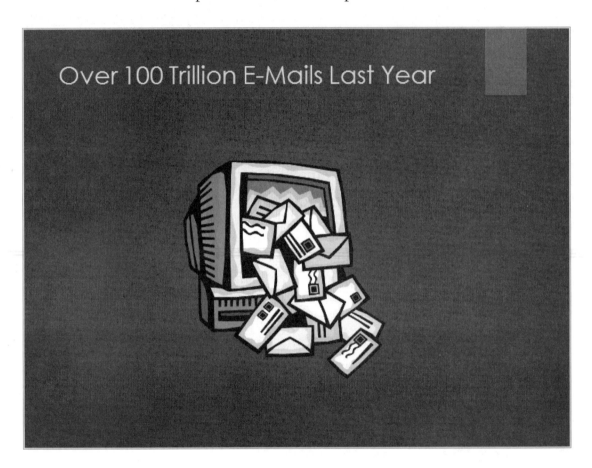

Presenting PowerPoint

PowerPoint 2013 is an intuitive, powerful presentation graphics program that enables you to create dynamic, multimedia presentations. You can deliver your presentation directly from your computer or by using an overhead video projection system.

PowerPoint lets you concentrate on the content of your presentation instead of focusing on design details. Using PowerPoint's built-in design themes, animations, and transitions, you can create highly effective, professional presentations. PowerPoint tools help you organize, develop, and deliver your presentation with precision, control, and creativity.

Starting PowerPoint

The method you use to start PowerPoint depends on whether you are using the Windows 7 or Windows 8 operating system.

- **Windows 7:** Click the Start button, choose Microsoft Office from the All Programs menu, and then choose PowerPoint 2013.

- **Windows 8:** Locate the PowerPoint 2013 tile on the Windows Start screen; click the tile to start PowerPoint.

After the PowerPoint program has started, click Blank Presentation to create a new blank presentation. To open an existing presentation:

- Start PowerPoint and choose a recent presentation. Or, choose Open Other Presentations, browse to a presentation, and double-click it.

- In either version of Windows, navigate to the desired document by using Windows Explorer or Computer and double-click the presentation.

HANDS-ON 7.1 **Start PowerPoint**

In this exercise, you will start PowerPoint.

1. Follow these steps for your version of Windows to open PowerPoint 2013:

Windows 7

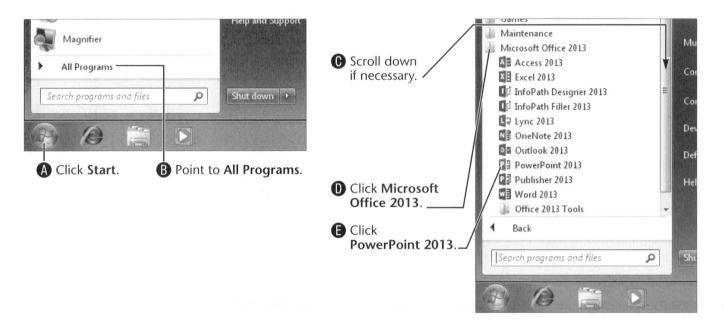

Ⓐ Click **Start.**

Ⓑ Point to **All Programs.**

Ⓒ Scroll down if necessary.

Ⓓ Click **Microsoft Office 2013.**

Ⓔ Click **PowerPoint 2013.**

Windows 8

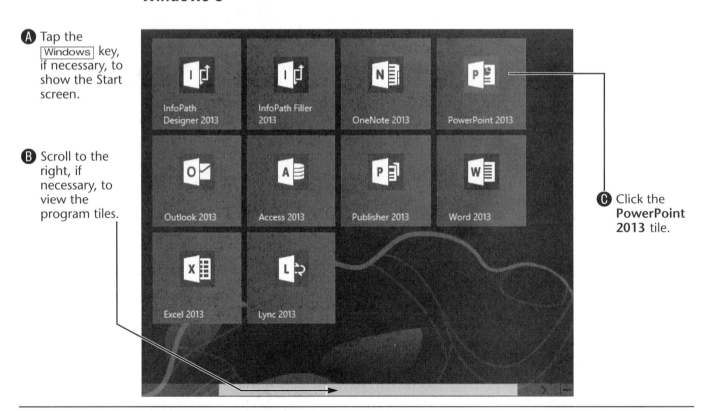

Ⓐ Tap the Windows key, if necessary, to show the Start screen.

Ⓑ Scroll to the right, if necessary, to view the program tiles.

Ⓒ Click the **PowerPoint 2013** tile.

Creating a New Presentation

When PowerPoint 2013 starts, it displays a Start screen that offers a variety of templates from which to choose. If your computer is connected to the Internet, PowerPoint will automatically display different templates every few times you start the program. A template is a blank presentation that is preformatted with matching graphics, colors, and fonts. If you aren't connected to the Internet, PowerPoint will display its default templates. A Blank Presentation option also is always available. Use it to create a blank, unformatted presentation to which you can add graphics, colors, and special fonts as you chose.

Recently opened presentations are displayed here.

Browse to open presentations on your computer.

Base your new presentation on a preformatted template.

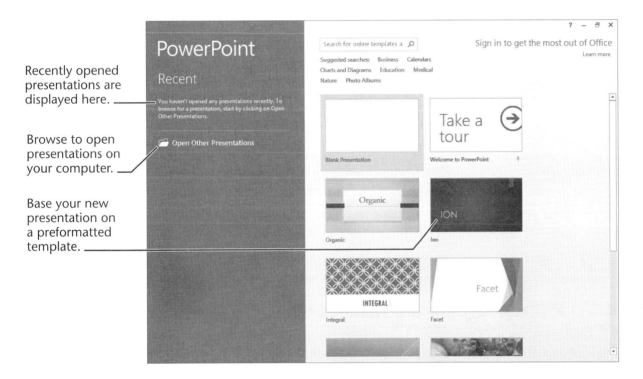

 HANDS-ON 7.2 **Create a Blank Presentation**

In this exercise, you will create a new, blank presentation.

1. Click the **Blank Presentation** template on the PowerPoint Start screen.

A new, blank presentation appears. You will develop it throughout this lesson.

The PowerPoint Window

The PowerPoint 2013 program window, like most other Microsoft Office programs, groups commands on the Ribbon. The following illustration provides an overview of the program window. Don't be concerned if your PowerPoint window looks slightly different from this example. The PowerPoint screen is customizable.

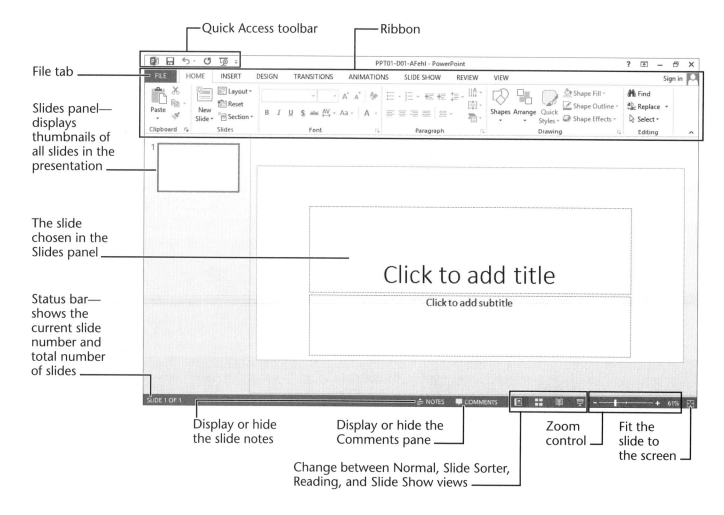

Navigating in a Presentation

PowerPoint has a number of features for navigating in a presentation. You can use both mouse techniques and keyboard techniques to move through a presentation. The technique you use is a matter of personal preference.

The Slides panel displays thumbnails of a presentation's slides. Clicking a thumbnail icon switches to that slide in the main window.

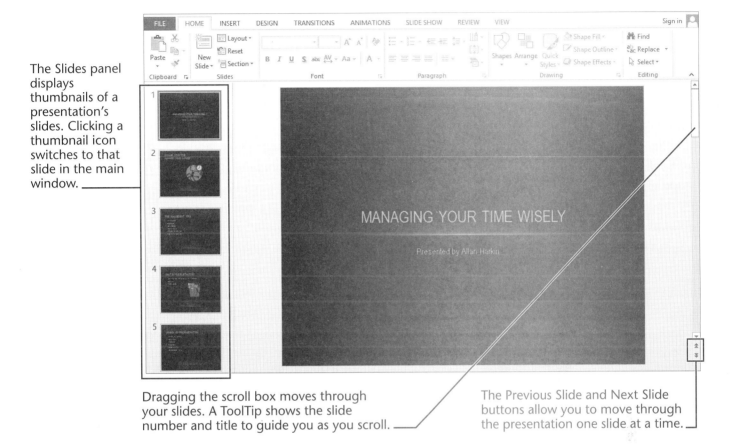

Dragging the scroll box moves through your slides. A ToolTip shows the slide number and title to guide you as you scroll.

The Previous Slide and Next Slide buttons allow you to move through the presentation one slide at a time.

QUICK REFERENCE: Navigating in PowerPoint

Task	Procedure
Move to the first slide	Drag the scroll box to the top of the scroll bar, or press Ctrl + Home .
Move to the last slide	Drag the scroll box to the bottom of the scroll bar, or press Ctrl + End .
Move to the next slide	Click Next Slide at the bottom of the scroll bar, or press PageDown .
Move to the previous slide	Click Previous Slide at the bottom of the scroll bar, or press PageUp .

Task	Procedure
Jump to a slide	Drag the scroll box and observe the ToolTip that displays the slide number and title, or click the desired thumbnail icon in the Slides tab.

 HANDS-ON 7.3 **Navigate in a Presentation**

In this exercise, you will navigate through a presentation using different methods, including both mouse and keyboard techniques.

1. Choose **File→Open→Computer→Browse** and open the **Time Management** presentation from your Lesson 07 folder.

2. Click the **slide 2** thumbnail icon in the Slides tab to switch to that slide.

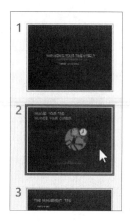

Slide 2 now appears in the Slide pane.

3. Follow these steps to use the tools in the scroll bar to navigate:

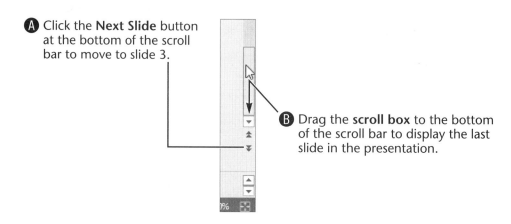

Ⓐ Click the **Next Slide** button at the bottom of the scroll bar to move to slide 3.

Ⓑ Drag the **scroll box** to the bottom of the scroll bar to display the last slide in the presentation.

4. Press Ctrl + Home to move to the beginning of the presentation.

5. Tap PageDown to move down one slide.

6. Press Ctrl+End to move to the last slide.

7. Drag the **scroll box** to the top of the scroll bar to return to slide 1.
   Leave the file open.

Using PowerPoint Views

You can view a presentation several ways. The views you will use in this lesson are easily accessible in the view bar, which is located at the bottom-right side of the screen.

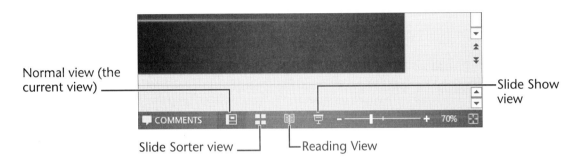

Normal view (the current view)

Slide Show view

Slide Sorter view

Reading View

The four views on the view bar include Normal (the view you have been using), Slide Sorter, Reading View, and Slide Show. Each view is described here.

- **Normal:** This is the primary view used when creating a presentation. It consists of three areas—the Slides pane on the left side of the screen, the Slide pane in the center of the screen, and the Notes pane at the bottom of the screen, where you can type speaker notes.

- **Slide Sorter:** This view displays all slides in miniature. It's a good way to get a helicopter view of your presentation. You can drag and drop slides with your mouse to rearrange them in Slide Sorter view.

- **Reading View:** With this view, the slide takes over the full PowerPoint screen but not the full Windows screen. The taskbar is still visible, so if you're working with several programs at once, for example, you can switch among programs using the taskbar.

- **Slide Show:** This is the view to use when you're ready to deliver your presentation. All slides take over the full Windows screen.

HANDS-ON 7.4 Explore PowerPoint Views

In this exercise, you will use the view bar to explore other views of a presentation. You will also rearrange slides in Slide Sorter view.

1. Click the **Slide Sorter** button on the view bar.

Your slides now look like thumbnails similar to those in the Slides panel on the left side of the screen in Normal view. Notice the highlighted border around slide 1. This indicates that slide 1 is active.

2. Click **slide 2** one time to make it active.

Notice that a highlighted border now surrounds slide 2.

Move Slides in Slide Sorter View

⚠ **TIP!** Slide Sorter view is one of the easiest views to use when you want to rearrange the order of your slides.

3. Follow these steps to move slide 4 to the left of slide 3:

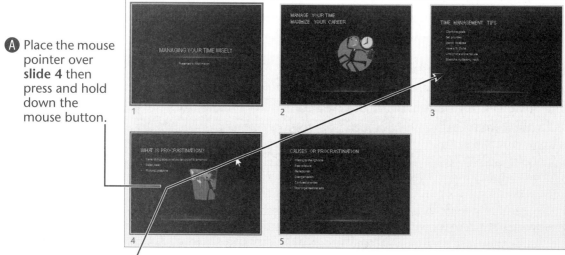

Ⓐ Place the mouse pointer over **slide 4** then press and hold down the mouse button.

Ⓑ Drag the mouse pointer between **slides 2 and 3**. The slides rearrange themselves as you drag.

Ⓒ Release the mouse button when **slide 4** is between **slides 2 and 3**.

4. Use the same technique to move **slide 5** between **slides 3 and 4**.

Use Slide Show View

5. Click **slide 1** to make it the active slide.

The active slide is the first slide that will appear when you click the Slide Show button.

6. Click the **Slide Show** button on the view bar.

7. Click the left mouse button to advance to the next slide.

8. Click the left mouse button three more times to move to the last slide.

9. Click the mouse button again and notice the all-black slide.

How did that get there? PowerPoint put it there for you. It's not a slide that you can see in Normal or Slide Sorter view. This slide gives the presenter an opportunity to wrap up the presentation without the audience looking at PowerPoint's Normal or Slide Sorter view. That would be distracting.

10. Click the mouse button again to return to Slide Sorter view.

You can see that this view would be distracting for the audience to look at while the presenter is wrapping up.

Use Reading View

11. If necessary, click **slide 1** to make it active.

12. Click the **Reading View** button.

You can see that this view covers the full PowerPoint window but that the Windows taskbar is still visible at the bottom of the screen. So, you can click a program icon on the taskbar to switch to another program, if necessary, while working in PowerPoint.

13. Click the left mouse button anywhere on the slide to advance to the next slide.

14. Continue clicking the left mouse button and notice the black slide at the end of the presentation—just as you saw in Slide Show view.

15. Click through the black slide to return to **Slide Sorter** view.

16. Click the **Normal** view button on the view bar.

17. Click **Save** 🖫 on the Quick Access toolbar.

18. Choose **File→Close** to close the presentation; leave PowerPoint open.

The Time Management presentation closes, and the blank presentation you created earlier displays.

Creating a Presentation

Now you will explore the exciting features that allow you to create powerful presentations effortlessly. You'll work with design themes, which add color and drama to your presentations, and with preformatted slide layouts, which make it easy to add text and graphics to your presentations.

As you add clip art to your presentation, you will find that working with clip art in PowerPoint is similar to working with clip art in Word. Once again, you are benefitting from the similarities among programs in a suite.

Using PowerPoint Themes

PowerPoint's built-in themes present professional-looking color schemes and background graphics at the click of a mouse. You can use Live Preview with themes to explore how various themes look before you apply them.

In addition, themes provide a consistent look throughout the presentation in terms of colors, fonts, and other design elements. Themes can also help set the mood for a presentation with their colors and graphic images. Easy-to-use themes allow you to concentrate your efforts on your message.

HANDS-ON 7.5   Use Themes in a Presentation

In this exercise, you will use Live Preview to explore PowerPoint's themes and apply a theme to your presentation.

1. Click the **Design** tab on the Ribbon and notice the Themes group.

2. Click the **More** button on the right side of the Themes gallery to display the entire gallery.

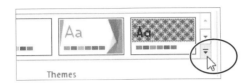

3. Hover the mouse pointer over several of the themes and watch as Live Preview displays samples of how the theme will look if you apply it to your slide.

   Notice that ToolTips displays the theme name when you hover the mouse pointer over a theme. Themes are listed in alphabetic order.

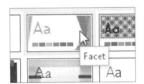

4. Use ToolTips to locate the **Wisp** theme.

5. Preview the theme for a moment and then click to apply it to the slide.

Save the Presentation

6. Choose **File→Save As**.

7. Click the **Browse** button at the bottom of the right column.

8. Navigate to the Lesson 07 folder in the Save As dialog box.

9. Type **Efficient Email** in the File Name box at the bottom of the dialog box, and then click **Save**.

Typing Text in a Slide

Slides contain dotted boxes called *placeholders*. Placeholders can contain text or objects such as tables, graphs, clip art, and other elements. For now you will concentrate on adding text to the title and subtitle placeholders in your title slide.

 HANDS-ON 7.6 **Add Text to a Slide**

In this exercise, you will add text to your title slide.

1. Click the **Click to Add Title** text placeholder.

   The placeholder is now selected and its handles (small squares) are visible. You can also see the flashing insertion point, indicating that you can begin to type.

2. Type **Efficient Email** in the text placeholder.

   The appearance of the font is part of the Wisp theme.

3. Click in the **Click to Add Subtitle** placeholder.

4. Type **Presented by Alec Harkins**.

5. Save 💾 the presentation.

   You are now ready to add a new slide to your presentation.

Slide Layouts

Slide layouts vary based on the text and graphic placeholders embedded in the slide and based on the current theme. The Layout gallery offers different ways to organize your slide contents.

The slide you just completed has the Title Slide layout, which contains title and subtitle placeholders. Next you will use a slide with the Title and Content layout, which contains a title placeholder and a content placeholder.

Title placeholder ——

Content placeholder ——

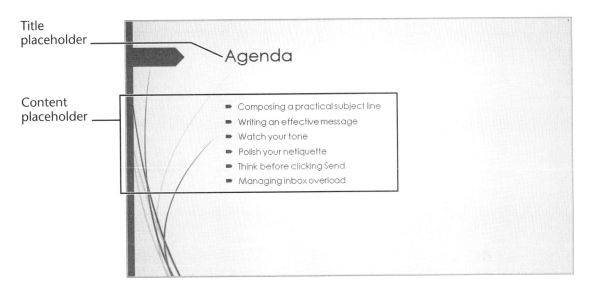

 HANDS-ON 7.7 **Add a Slide and Try Different Layouts**

In this exercise, you will add a slide and apply different layouts from the Layout gallery.

1. Choose **Home→Slides→New Slide** .

A new slide is added to the presentation using the default Title and Content layout. Notice the icons that appear in the bottom placeholder. You can click these icons to add elements such as tables, charts, and pictures to the slide.

Change the Slide Layout

The Layout gallery does not use Live Preview, so you have to apply a layout to your slide to see its effect.

2. Choose **Home→Slides→** Layout ▾ .

3. Click **Section Header**.

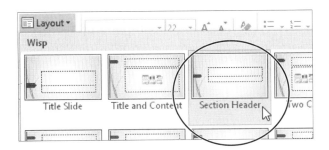

4. Choose **Home**→**Slides**→ ⊞ Layout ▾ .

5. Click the **Two Content** layout.
   Feel free to test other layouts if you wish.

6. Choose **Home**→**Slides**→ ⊞ Layout ▾ .

7. Apply the **Title and Content** layout.

8. **Save** 💾 the presentation.

Presentation Design Tips

You are now ready to add more content to your presentation. Following are some tried-and-true recommendations from professional presenters. Keeping these guidelines in mind goes a long way in helping you design your presentation like a pro.

Don't Write an Essay   People glaze over when they see dense text. Slide content should provide a roadmap of main points for the presenter.

• Use a maximum of eight lines per slide.

• If there's a lot of information, break up the lines over a few slides.

• Don't write in complete sentences; just hit the high points.

Font   It's fun to play with different fonts, but keeping it simple is the recommendation for presentations.

• Size should be at least 18 points. If possible, go to the back of the room where the presentation will take place and see if you can read the slides.

• Limit the number of fonts to about three per presentation; that includes point size changes.

• Sticking with the fonts the theme provides is a good recommendation.

Design Theme   Most people recommend a design theme with a dark background, as they are typically more visually appealing, but a dark background can look faded if the room is too light. If possible, check the room conditions first. Also, keep in mind that it's easier on the eyes to read black text on a white (or light) background.

Special Effects   Again, think simple. Special effects like clip art, animations, and slide transitions are fun, but they can detract from your message. Use special effects to emphasize a point, never to entertain.

HANDS-ON 7.8 Add Content to Your New Slide

In this exercise, you will add text to the title placeholder and the content placeholder.

1. Click the title placeholder and type **Agenda**.

2. Click the bottom placeholder and type this text:

   `Compose a practical subject line`

   `Write an effective message`

   `Watch your tone`

   `Polish your netiquette`

   `Think before clicking Send`

   `Learn to manage inbox overload`

3. Save 🖫 the presentation.

Adding Clip Art

You can search for and insert clip art from the Internet directly from within PowerPoint. Adding clip art will help you emphasize key points and add polish to the presentation as a whole. The Microsoft Office website has a clip art collection of more than 130,000 pieces of art—and it grows daily. There is clip art available for any occasion.

While the term *clip art* is an industry standard term referring to pre-drawn artwork added to computer documents, Microsoft uses the terms *clip art* and *online pictures* inconsistently to refer to the same thing. For example, PowerPoint's Online Pictures button opens the Insert Pictures dialog box, which allows you to search the Office.com web site for clip art.

The Insert Pictures Search Window

The Insert Pictures search window replaces the Clip Art panel that existed in previous PowerPoint versions. This new window lets you search for clip art on the Office.com Clip Art website or from the Bing™ search engine. Each piece of clip art is associated with keywords that describe its characteristics. For example, the images shown can be located by using the keyword *awards* or *prizes*.

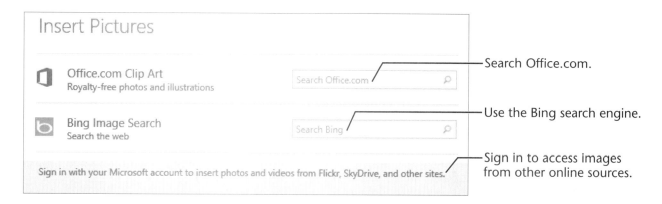

Search Office.com.

Use the Bing search engine.

Sign in to access images from other online sources.

Begin a new search from a different search engine.

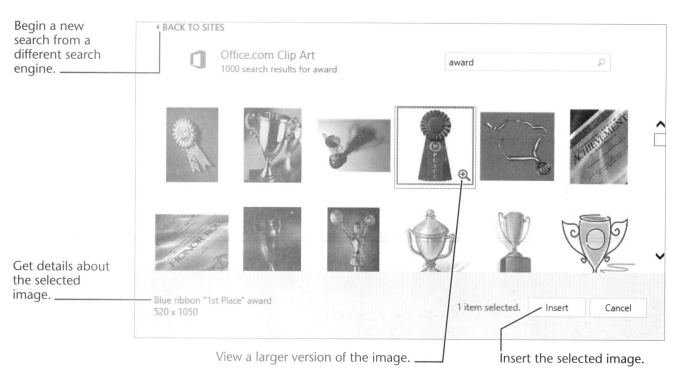

Get details about the selected image.

View a larger version of the image.

Insert the selected image.

HANDS-ON 7.9 Add Clip Art to the Presentation

In this exercise, you will add a new slide containing a clip art icon embedded in it. You will use the icon to open the Insert Pictures dialog box. Then you will search for a clip art image related to email and insert it in the slide.

1. Choose **Home→Slides→New Slide menu button ▾**.

   This displays the Layout gallery where you can select the layout *before* inserting the slide.

2. Choose the **Title and Content** layout.

3. Click the title placeholder and type **Over 100 Trillion Emails Last Year**.

4. Click the **Online Pictures** icon in the bottom placeholder.

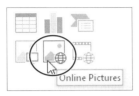

The Insert Pictures dialog box opens.

5. Follow these steps to search for clip art:

A Type **email** in the Office.com search box.

B Tap Enter.

6. Follow these steps to insert a picture on the slide:

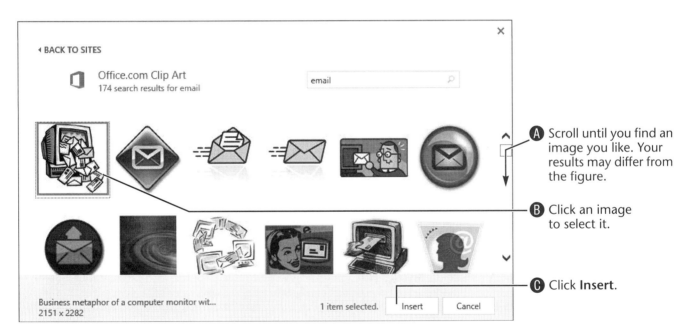

A Scroll until you find an image you like. Your results may differ from the figure.

B Click an image to select it.

C Click **Insert**.

The clip art image is inserted on the slide and replaces the large text box.

Move the Clip Art

7. Hover the mouse pointer over the image. When the mouse pointer changes to a four-headed arrow, drag up and to the left a couple of inches and then release the mouse button.

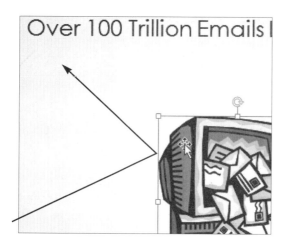

As you drag, PowerPoint displays dashed red lines to help you align the picture to other items on the slide, such as the title.

Resize the Clip Art

8. Place the mouse pointer over the bottom-right corner handle, and when the pointer changes to a double-headed arrow, drag down and to the right to enlarge the image.

9. Release the mouse button.

10. Adjust the size and position of the image as you deem necessary.

11. Save your presentation.

Delivering the Slide Show

The slides are created, and the presentation is complete. The first phase is over. The next phase, delivering the presentation, is just beginning. The successful communication of the presentation is dependent on the presenter.

The PowerPoint slide show is secondary to the message the presenter is delivering, and the manner in which you convey the message is critical to grabbing the audience's attention and keeping it. Before you stand in front of an audience, familiarize yourself with the following tips.

Delivery Tips

It's not only *what* you say, it's *how* you say it that makes the difference between an engaging and an unsuccessful presentation. Lead your audience. Help them focus on the message of your presentation. Use the following PEER guidelines to deliver effective presentations.

- **Pace:** Maintain a moderate pace. Speaking too fast will exhaust your audience and speaking too slowly may put them to sleep. Carry your audience with you as you talk.

- **Emphasis:** Pause for emphasis. As you present, use a brief pause to emphasize your points. Pausing gives your audience time to absorb your message.

- **Eye Contact:** Always face your audience while speaking. A common mistake is to speak while walking or facing the projection screen. Don't waste all of the work you have done in PowerPoint by losing your audience's interest now. If you are speaking from a lectern, resist the temptation to lean on it. Stand tall and look directly at your audience.

- **Relax:** You are enthusiastic and want to convey that tone. However, when you speak, avoid fast movements, pacing, and rushed talking. Your audience will be drawn to your movements and miss the point. Remember that the audience is listening to you to learn; this material may be old hat to you, but it's new to them. Speak clearly, maintain a steady pace, and stay calm.

Navigating in Slide Show View

You use different navigation techniques in a slide show than the ones you used in Normal view. There are several methods you can use to move through a slide show. They include using the mouse, the keyboard, and the Slide Show toolbar.

Using the Mouse and the Keyboard   The following Quick Reference table provides mouse and keyboard techniques for moving through a presentation in Slide Show view.

QUICK REFERENCE: Navigating in a Slide Show

Task	Procedure
Advance a slide	Click once with the mouse, or tap Spacebar, →, PageDown, or Enter.

Task	Procedure
Back up a slide	Tap [Backspace], [PageUp], or [←].
Display the Slide Show toolbar	Move the mouse around on the screen for a moment.

Navigate with the Slide Show Toolbar   The Slide Show toolbar is your navigator during the slide show. It's hidden when a slide show starts, but becomes visible when you move your mouse around or point to the lower-left area of the screen. The Slide Show toolbar can be used to navigate a slide show or to draw attention to a specific area on a slide. However, use of this toolbar is unnecessary when you present a simple slide show like this one.

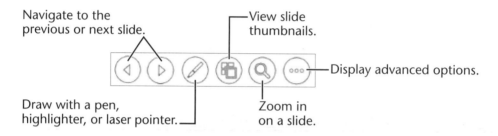

Navigate to the previous or next slide.

View slide thumbnails.

Display advanced options.

Draw with a pen, highlighter, or laser pointer.

Zoom in on a slide.

 HANDS-ON 7.10   Run the Slide Show

In this exercise, you will use various techniques to navigate in your slide show.

1. Follow these steps to start the slide show:

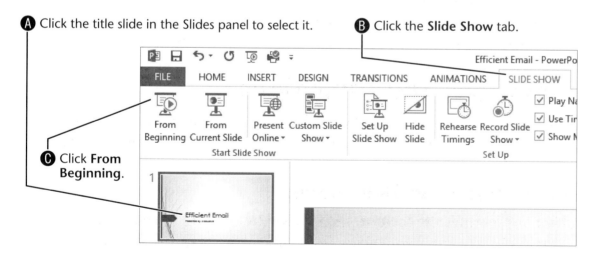

Ⓐ Click the title slide in the Slides panel to select it.

Ⓑ Click the **Slide Show** tab.

Ⓒ Click **From Beginning**.

2. Move the mouse pointer around the screen for a moment.

Notice the Slide Show ⊲ ▷ ✎ ▦ ⊕ ⦿ toolbar that appears near the bottom-left corner of the screen when the slides are in full-screen view.

3. Click the mouse pointer anywhere on the screen to move to the next slide.

4. Tap PageDown and then tap PageUp twice using the keys near the main keyboard (not the keys on the numeric keypad).

PowerPoint displays the next or previous slide each time you tap these keys.

5. Follow these steps to use the Slide Show toolbar:

Ⓐ Point to the lower-left area of the slide to display the Slide Show toolbar.

Ⓑ Click **Show all Slides** to display thumbnails of all slides.

⊲ ▷ ✎ ▦ ⊕ ⦿

6. Click the **Agenda** slide.

As you can see, there are many ways to navigate slides in a slide show.

End the Slide Show

7. Continue to click anywhere on the screen until the last slide appears (the Over 100 Trillion slide).

8. Click once on the last slide.

The screen turns to a black background, with a small note at the top.

9. Click anywhere on the black screen to exit the slide show and return to the main PowerPoint window.

Next you will really jazz things up by adding animations and transitions.

Adding Animations and Transitions

Now that you have completed your slides and run a slide show, you decide to liven up the show using PowerPoint's animations and transitions features.

Animating Your Slide Show

Animation brings life to your presentation by affecting how text or objects, such as clip art, enter your slide. Following are a few buttons from the Animation group on the Ribbon to give you an idea of the possibilities.

If you have lines of text in the Content placeholder, you can have them fade, fly, or float into your slide when you click the mouse button. This keeps your audience focused on the point you are discussing.

 HANDS-ON 7.11 **Animate a Slide**

In this exercise, you will add life to your slides by applying animations. You will test several different animation options.

1. If necessary, click **slide 2** in the Slides pane to display it.

2. Click anywhere in the bottom placeholder to make it active.

3. Choose **Animations→Animation→Fly In** ⭐.

   Wow, pretty interesting! Notice the items are numbered 1 through 6. This is the order in which the items will appear in the slide show when you click the mouse button. Now you will check out how that works in Slide Show view.

4. Click the **Slide Show** 🖳 button on the View Bar toward the bottom-right corner of the screen.

5. Click the mouse button to see the first point fly into the slide.

6. Click the mouse button to see the second point fly into the slide.

   Can you see how that keeps the audience focused on what the presenter is talking about?

7. Keep clicking the mouse button to see all of the items fly into the slide. The last slide, Over 100 Trillion, displays.

8. Tap Esc to end the slide show.

Try Out More Animations

9. Make sure the second slide is active, and then click in the bottom placeholder.

10. Choose **Animations→Animation→More**.

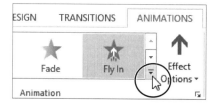

11. Click **Wipe** to apply and preview that animation.

12. Choose **Animations→Animation→More** and take a few moments to test other animations.

13. When you find an animation you like, apply it to the slide and then try it out in **Slide Show** view.

14. End the slide show and return to **Normal** view.

15. Save your presentation.

Adding Transitions

Transitions are like the six o'clock news effects. When the news commentator finishes one story and transitions to the next, there is typically some type of graphic effect that leads to the next story.

Following are a few of the buttons located in the Transition to This Slide group on the Ribbon. You can have a wipe, split, or reveal effect when moving from one slide to another in your presentation.

 HANDS-ON 7.12 **Add Transitions**

In this exercise, you will test out some transition effects. When you find a transition you like, you will check it out in Slide Show view.

1. If necessary, make **slide 1** the active slide.

2. Choose **Transitions→Transition to This Slide→Split** .

3. Choose **Transitions→Transition to This Slide→Wipe** .

4. Take a few moments to test some other transitions.

5. When you find the transition you like, switch to **slide 2** and apply the transition.

6. Switch to **slide 3** and apply the transition.

   Although you could apply a different transition to each slide, it would likely be distracting for the audience if you did. Some of PowerPoint's transitions are pretty lively and possibly distracting. Think "subtle" when selecting a transition.

7. Make **slide 1** active, and then check out your presentation in **Slide Show** view.

8. Save and close your presentation.

Concepts Review

To check your knowledge of the key concepts introduced in this lesson, complete the Concepts Review quiz here. Or, take the quiz online by going to the student resource center.

True/False Questions

Page number

1. You can use Live Preview with themes to explore how themes look before applying them.   **true**   **false**   _____

2. Themes provide a consistent look throughout a presentation in terms of colors, fonts, and other design elements.   **true**   **false**   _____

3. The Slide Show toolbar provides the only methods for navigating in a slide show.   **true**   **false**   _____

4. You can add only clip art pictures that you already have on your hard drive.   **true**   **false**   _____

5. Animation affects how text or objects enter your slide.   **true**   **false**   _____

6. You use Slide Sorter view when you're ready to deliver a presentation.   **true**   **false**   _____

Multiple Choice Questions

7. Which view displays the presentation in the full Windows screen?

Page number: _____

a. Normal

b. Slide Show

c. Reading View

d. Slide Sorter

8. Which of the following *is not* a method of navigating through a presentation in Normal view?

Page number: _____

a. Dragging the scroll box

b. Using the Slide Show toolbar

c. Using the Slides tab

d. Using the Next Side and Previous Slide buttons on the scroll bar

9. Which of the following *is not* a slide layout?

Page number: _____

a. Title and Content

b. Title Slide

c. Blank

d. Clip Art

10. Which of the following views *is not* available on the view bar?

Page number: _____

a. Print Preview

b. Slide Sorter

c. Normal

d. Slide Show

Skill Builders

SKILL BUILDER 7.1 ### Present the Giraffes

Your niece, Leona, hears about your giraffe graph and is intrigued! She has asked you to come to her school to give a presentation on giraffes. In this exercise, you will use the picture icon embedded in a slide to insert a photograph of the giraffes. Then you will copy your giraffe graph into the presentation.

1. Choose **File→New**.

2. Click **Blank Presentation**.

   ### Apply a Theme

3. Click the **Design** tab.

4. Click the **More** button on the right side of the Themes gallery to display the entire gallery.

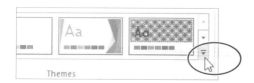

5. Apply the **Organic** theme to the slide.
   Remember, the themes are in alphabetic order.

6. Click the title placeholder and type **My Trip to the Zoo**.

7. Click the subtitle placeholder and type **By Leona Goodspeed**.

   ### Add a New Slide and Insert a Photograph

8. Choose **Home→Slides→New Slide** 🔲.

9. Click in the title placeholder and type **The Giraffes**.

10. Click the **Pictures** icon.

11. Navigate to your Lesson 07 folder and double-click **sb-Giraffe Picture**.

Add a New Slide and Change the Layout

12. Choose **Home**→**Slides**→**New Slide** ▥.

13. Choose **Home**→**Slides**→▥ Layout ▾.

14. Choose the **Title Only** layout.

15. Click the title placeholder and type **Graph of Giraffe Heights**.

16. Save the presentation as **sb-My Trip to the Zoo**.

Next you will copy a graph from an Excel file. You haven't switched between software programs before, so saving at this point is just an extra precaution.

Start Excel and Copy a Graph into the Slide

17. Start **Excel**.

18. Click ▱ **Open Other Workbooks** in the bottom of the left pane.

19. Click ▱ Computer in the middle column.

20. Click ▱ Browse in the right column.

21. Navigate to your Lesson 07 folder and double-click **sb-Giraffe Graph**.

22. If a yellow bar appears across the top of the Excel window indicating a Security Warning or that the spreadsheet was opened in Protected View, click **Enable Content** or **Enable Editing** (whichever displays) to allow copying of the chart.

23. If a message appears indicating that some links in the workbook cannot be updated, click **Continue**.

24. Click the outside border of the graph to select it.

25. Choose **Home**→**Clipboard**→**Copy** ▥.

26. Click the **PowerPoint** icon on the Windows taskbar to switch to PowerPoint.

27. Choose **Home**→**Clipboard**→**Paste** ▥.

The graph appears in the slide, but it's a little too big. You'll resize the graph next.

Resize and Move the Graph

28. Position the mouse pointer in the upper-left corner of the graph frame and notice that the pointer changes to a double-headed arrow.

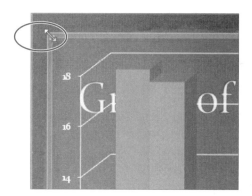

29. Press and hold down the mouse button, and drag down and to the right until the graph is below the title.

    The graph is not perfectly centered on the slide.

30. Position the mouse pointer in the bottom-center of the graph frame and notice that the pointer changes to a double-headed arrow.

31. Press and hold down the mouse button, and drag up until the graph fits in the white area of the slide without overlapping the border.

32. Position the mouse pointer on the border of the graph frame so the pointer changes to a four-headed arrow.

33. Press and hold down the mouse button, and drag a little to the left until the graph is well-centered on the slide; release the mouse button.

34. Make **slide 1** active; check out your presentation in Slide Show view.

35. Save and close the presentation.

36. Click the **Excel** icon on the taskbar to restore the Excel window.

37. Click the X in the top-right corner of the Excel window.

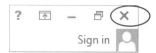

Add Animation and Transitions to a Presentation

In this exercise, you will open a presentation and add some pizzazz with animation and transitions.

1. Open **sb-Tropical Getaways** from your Lesson 07 folder.

2. Click the **slide 2** thumbnail icon in the Slides panel on the left side of the screen.

   Notice that slide 2 contains bullet points. That's part of the design for the Facet theme used in this presentation.

Add Animation to a Slide

3. Click in the bottom-left placeholder to select it.

   You now see a dotted-line box surrounding the placeholder.

4. Choose **Animations→Animation→Fade** ⭐.

   Notice during the preview that each item fades in separately, one after the other.

5. Switch to **Slide Show** 🖥 view and click the mouse button four times to display each of the first four destinations.

   Hmmm, that seems a little tedious. It might be better if the four destinations appeared at the same time.

6. Right-click a blank area of the slide and choose **End Slideshow**.

   ⚠ **TIP!** If you select (highlight) all four of the items and then apply the animation, they will behave as one unit.

7. Place the **I-beam** Ɪ mouse pointer to the left of the *T* in *Tahiti* and drag down to select all four destinations.

8. Choose **Animations→Animation→Fade** ⭐.

   Notice during the preview that all four items fade in together as one unit.

9. Switch to **Slide Show** 🖥 view; click the mouse button once and all four items display at the same time.

10. End the slide show.

11. Drag to select all four items in the bottom-right placeholder and apply the **Fade** animation.

Apply Animation to Additional Slides

12. Switch to **slide 3**.

13. Click in the bottom-left placeholder to select it.

14. Choose **Animations→Animation→Fly In** ⭐.

    Notice that during the preview all four items fly in together. How did that happen when you didn't select all four items first? It's because the last three items are sub bullets (indented) below the main bullet. That causes PowerPoint to assume that the items should act as one unit. (You create sub-bullets in a placeholder by pressing the Tab key.)

15. Click in the bottom-right placeholder to select it and apply the **Fly In** animation.

16. Go to **slide 4**, click the bottom placeholder, and apply the **Float In** animation. (You may have to use the More button in the Animation group.)

    This time PowerPoint assumes that each of the main bullets and their associated sub-bullets are a unit. You have two main bullets, so each one floats in with its associated sub-bullets.

17. Go to **slide 5** and apply the animation of your choice to the bulleted text.

18. Tap Ctrl+Home to return to the beginning of the presentation.

19. Switch to **Slide Show** view and enjoy the show.

    Remember, it's fun to play with different animations, but you don't want to distract the audience. For actual business-related presentations, consider using only one or two animation styles for the entire show.

Add Transitions to the Slide Show

Using a variety of transitions could be distracting, so you will apply the same transition to all slides. Using Slide Sorter view is an easy way to apply the same transition to all slides at the same time.

20. Click the **Slide Sorter** ⊞ icon in the bottom-right corner of the window.

21. If necessary, click **slide 1** to make it active.

    It will have a highlighted border around it if it's active.

    TIP! If you select a slide and then hold the Shift key and click another slide, PowerPoint also selects all the slides in between.

22. Hold down Shift and click **slide 6**; release the Shift key.

    All six slides now have a highlighted border, meaning all six slides are selected.

23. Choose **Transitions→Transition to This Slide→Push** .

View Your Final Presentation

24. Click **slide 1** to reselect slide 1 and deselect the other slides.

25. Switch to **Slide Show** view and run the slide show.

26. Save and close the presentation.

27. Click the **X** in the top-right corner of the **PowerPoint** window to close PowerPoint.

Access – Accessing Raritan Clinic East

Have you ever wondered how service agents who take your order over the telephone know what questions to ask about the products you order...or how sportscasters come up with little-known facts about teams and players in a flash? In most cases, these service agents and sportscasters have access to a powerful database from which they obtain the information.

In this lesson, you will explore elements of the Microsoft Access 2013 application window, create a new database, and identify features of the database window. As you explore the tools available in Access 2013, you will begin building the new database.

LEARNING OBJECTIVES

After studying this lesson, you will be able to:

- Launch Access 2013 and identify elements of the application window

- Create a new blank database and database table

- Use the Navigation Pane and enter data into a table

- Save and close database objects

- Preview and print datasheets

- Close a database and exit Access 2013

Case Study: Creating the Raritan Clinic East Table and Database

Raritan Clinic East is an incorporated medical practice staffed by the finest clinical diagnosticians in the pediatric fields of general medicine, cardiology, orthopedics, pediatrics, emergency medicine, and neonatology. The practice serves a patient community ranging in age from newborn to eighteen years old.

James Elliott has recently accepted a position in the Raritan Clinic East Human Resources Department. He has been tasked with reviewing the current records management system. From this review, he will be able to determine how best to organize data in new databases created using Access 2013. Then he will create a new database in which to store the data so that information can be located and retrieved more efficiently.

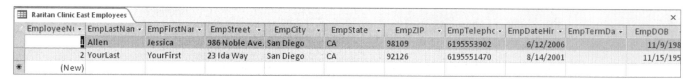

The table created to hold employee data

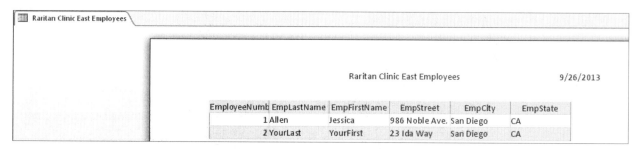

A printout of data from the new database table

Defining Access Databases

If you have ever used a phone book or a catalog, retrieved a note card from a card file, or pulled a file from a file cabinet, you have used a paper-based database. If you have ever used an index or a table of contents in a book, you have also used a database—just a different type of database. Each of these items consists of individual pieces of *data* that, when combined, make up a *database*.

What Is a Database?

A *database* is a collection of related data stored together in one electronic file. Historically, individuals and businesses have used databases to store vast amounts of data in an organized fashion to facilitate quick and easy retrieval of facts, figures, and information. Prior to the computer age, database records were stored on index cards, on columnar tablets, and in file folders stored in file cabinets. While these data storage methods are still around today, computer-based (electronic) databases have reduced the storage requirements of data and have improved the efficiency of data retrieval. As a result, reports from sportscasters, historians, politicians, stock sales, unemployment records, and many other details can be reported with amazing accuracy—and very quickly.

Exploring the Access Environment

When you launch Access 2013, one of the first things you will notice is that, unlike other Microsoft Office applications, Access displays the Backstage view rather than a new blank file. From the Access startup screen, you can create a new database or open an existing one.

Starting Access

The basic procedures for launching Access 2013 are the same as those used to launch other Microsoft Office applications. After you launch Access, you may open or create a database, search for an online database template, or create a custom web app.

These procedures may vary somewhat, depending on the version of Windows installed on your computer, as well as whether Access has been used on the computer previously.

HANDS-ON 8.1A Launch Access 2013 (Windows 8)

Windows 7 Users: Skip this exercise.

In this exercise, you will start the Access 2013 program.

1. If necessary, start your computer.

   The Windows Start screen appears.

2. Locate the **Access 2013** tile.

3. Click the tile to start Access.

   The Access program loads, and the Access Start screen appears.

4. Make sure the Access window is **maximized** ▢.

   After you launch Access for the first time, you may want to pin the Access 2013 application to the taskbar.

HANDS-ON 8.1B Launch Access 2013 (Windows 7)

Windows 8 Users: Skip this exercise.

In this exercise, you will launch Access 2013 from the Start menu.

1. From the Desktop, click the **Start** 🞂 button.

2. Choose **All Programs**.

3. Click the **Microsoft Office** folder.

4. Choose **Microsoft Access 2013**.

   After you launch Access for the first time, you may want to pin the Access 2013 application to the Start screen or to the taskbar. You can launch Access directly from the Start screen instead of searching for it each time.

Identifying Elements of the Access Window

Access, unlike other Microsoft Office applications, displays the Backstage view when you launch the application. From this screen, you can choose to create a custom web app or a blank desktop database, search for online templates, or open other files.

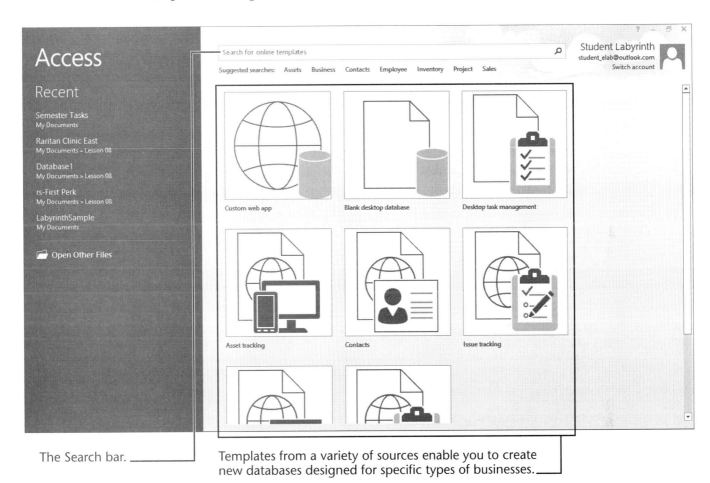

The Search bar.

Templates from a variety of sources enable you to create new databases designed for specific types of businesses.

Custom Web Apps

You can use Access 2013 to build a custom web app to share in a web browser. Once you determine the app name, web location, and type of data (i.e., contacts, events, etc.), Access automatically creates the database shell and object types (i.e., table, form). You can then add and modify your data.

Blank Desktop Databases

An electronic database file serves as a shell that holds all the tools, data, and database objects that help users enter and organize data and obtain meaningful information from that data. As a result, you must save the empty database shell and give it a name before you create it.

An Access 2013 database created using the Blank desktop database button has the default filename of Database1 and is stored to a file location on the hard drive in the user's account. You can change both the filename and the file location. After you create a new database, Access automatically creates a blank table named Table1.

An Access database has various objects, including tables, queries, forms, and reports. Each object type can be created from scratch using a Design View for the particular type of object. Access also provides wizards to help you set up individual objects. You will use the Database View as you develop the database in this lesson.

Designing a Database

The first step in designing any database is to determine the type of information you will need to store in it. Examples of data include the names, addresses, telephone numbers, and email addresses of customers or contacts. Once the needed information has been determined, you can design the database to accommodate it. A database structure can be changed, but modifications to the structure should be kept at a minimum to prevent unwanted data loss. Sometimes changing the structure can corrupt or delete data that has already been entered. This is why it is important to begin with a good design.

HANDS-ON 8.2 Create a Blank Database

In this exercise, you will create a new blank database named Raritan Clinic East.

1. Follow these steps to create and name the new database:

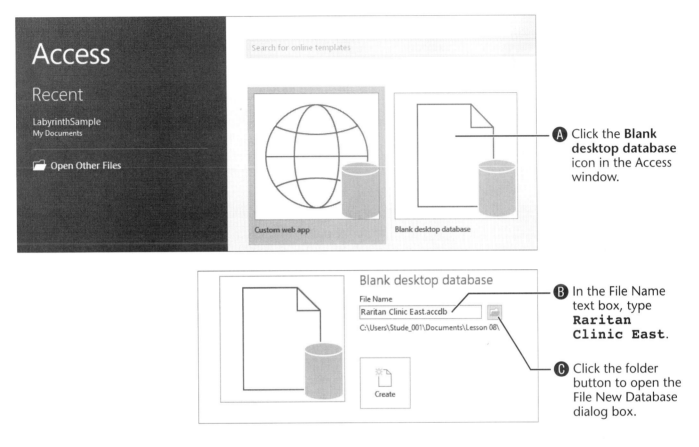

A Click the **Blank desktop database** icon in the Access window.

B In the File Name text box, type **Raritan Clinic East**.

C Click the folder button to open the File New Database dialog box.

2. Navigate to the **Lesson 08** folder or the folder in which you want to store your files and click **OK**.

3. Click the **Create** button.

Access creates the new database, shows the database name in the application title bar, and displays a blank table named Table1 in the Access window.

Identifying Features of the Database Window

Now that you have created the database file, take a moment to study the Datasheet View layout of the window and to compare the visual elements of the window with the features you have seen in other Microsoft Office applications.

The Navigation Pane appears on the left side of the window.

Tabs on the Ribbon display Access tools.

The title bar shows the database name and the file location where the database is stored.

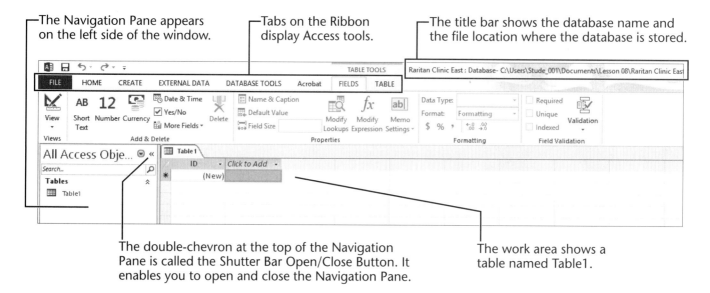

The double-chevron at the top of the Navigation Pane is called the Shutter Bar Open/Close Button. It enables you to open and close the Navigation Pane.

The work area shows a table named Table1.

The Navigation Pane

If you have used Microsoft Office Excel, you know that navigating within a worksheet or workbook is different from navigating within paragraphs of a document. Navigating within an Access database is also different from navigating in a document. As you begin working with the database, some basic procedures for using the Navigation Pane will enable you to navigate the file more efficiently.

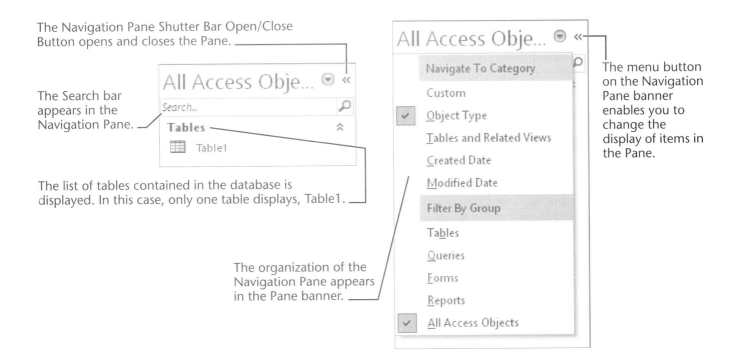

The Navigation Pane Shutter Bar Open/Close Button opens and closes the Pane.

The Search bar appears in the Navigation Pane.

The list of tables contained in the database is displayed. In this case, only one table displays, Table1.

The organization of the Navigation Pane appears in the Pane banner.

The menu button on the Navigation Pane banner enables you to change the display of items in the Pane.

Creating Tables in Datasheet View

All data stored in a database is stored in tables. As a result, Access creates a table for each new database you create, identifies the object using a generic table number (Table1), and creates one field (ID). Access also displays the Table Tools Fields and Table Ribbons so that the tools you need as you build the first table are available. When a database object is active, Access automatically places new Ribbon tabs at the right end of the Tab bar to make accessing appropriate tools more efficient.

Table Tools are distributed on two tabs.

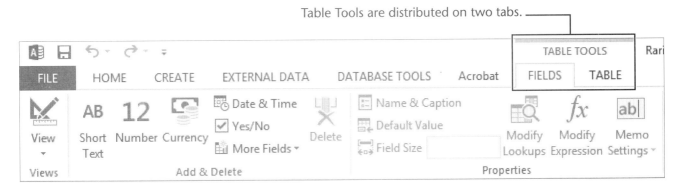

Before you begin building your first table, there are some terms and rules you need to know about tables.

Working with Tables

A database table is the basic object of any database because tables store all of the raw data placed into the database. All other objects in a database are based on data stored in tables. In most databases, you will find a number of tables, each of which holds data related in some way to data in other tables in the database.

Three key terms are used in relation to the data stored in Access databases.

- **Field:** The basic unit of database tables that holds one piece of data, such as first name, last name, street address, ZIP code, date of birth, and so forth. Notice that name fields of first name and last name are separated into two fields. Each field appears as a table column that you read down the screen.

- **Record:** A collection of all fields related to one item, such as all fields of data for one person, one order, or one place. Each record appears in a table row that goes across the screen.

- **File:** A collection of all related records stored together, such as all employee records found in a table, all customers, all suppliers, and so forth. Each field and record in a database table—along with forms, reports, and queries used to input data and retrieve meaningful information—make up a database file.

Tables are most commonly displayed in Datasheet View, which presents data from multiple records in the column/row layout shown in Table1. As you review the following sample table and work with tables, you will see how these elements fit together.

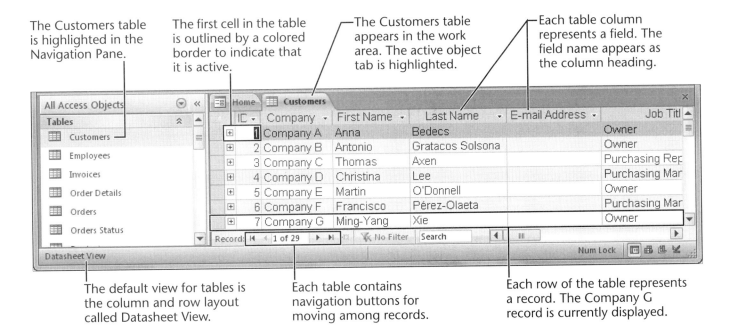

The Customers table is highlighted in the Navigation Pane.

The first cell in the table is outlined by a colored border to indicate that it is active.

The Customers table appears in the work area. The active object tab is highlighted.

Each table column represents a field. The field name appears as the column heading.

The default view for tables is the column and row layout called Datasheet View.

Each table contains navigation buttons for moving among records.

Each row of the table represents a record. The Company G record is currently displayed.

Table Guidelines

If you are acquainted with the Microsoft Word table feature or Microsoft Excel worksheets, you will find using the Access datasheet familiar. Because tables hold the field names and data used in other database objects, tables must be created first in Access databases.

Each table in the Raritan Clinic East database will contain fields that focus on specific data—patients, supplies, employees, etc. As you build the tables for the database, consider these guidelines:

- Each table should have a *primary key* field that contains unique data—data that is not the same for any two records. Social security numbers are a good example of unique data because no two people have the same number. However, many organizations avoid using social security numbers for security reasons and, instead, use some type of coded ID such as employee number, patient number, or item number as primary keys.

- The field identified as the primary key field must contain data; it cannot be empty. When Access creates the primary key field, it automatically sets the key field to number the records. This ensures that each record has a unique number.

- As you have discovered in the database you just created, Access generates the first field (ID) for you. It uses this field as a primary key field designed to hold unique data. To ensure that the data is unique, Access will assign sequential numeric values to each record you enter. You can leave the field with the predefined Access numbers in sequence, you can change the ID, or you can change the ID field to a different field name and type, depending on how your table is set up.

- Planning the layout of the database tables, including the type of data to display, before you add them to the database reduces the amount of time spent editing and restructuring the tables later. It's also helpful to have an idea of what the final reports should look like. Be sure to talk with the people entering the data from a paper-based form, as well as those who will be reviewing the final reports.

- In order to connect, or relate, data from two or more tables to create reports and other database objects, the tables must have at least one field in common. These common fields are sometimes referred to as *foreign keys*. In an Employees table for example, the Employee ID Number field might relate to a similarly named field in another table. In the other table, the Customers table, for example, the Employee No field may contain the employee ID numbers of the employees who took the order. The two fields (Employee ID Number and Employee No) will serve as a foreign key so the tables can relate and share common data.

Reserved Words

Access contains a list of specific words that it considers *reserved* words. Reserved words have special meaning for Access or for the Microsoft database engine. If you use these words as field names or objects names, you may receive an error message. Reserved words may be used in conjunction with other words as field names as long as the reserved word is connected without spaces to another word in the field name.

One example of a reserved word is the word *name*. This word cannot be used alone as a field name; it is reserved. It can, however, be used as part of another word, such as *FirstName*. You may want to do an Internet search for reserved words to obtain a complete list.

Field Data Types

As you access each column in a new table datasheet, Access displays a drop-down list that enables you to identify the type of data you plan to place in the field. When you think about the data you plan to enter for a field, it's easy to see the different types of data—text, currency, dates, and so forth. By defining the type of data each field will contain, Access formats the data to some degree, and reduces the amount of formatting you must apply as you enter the data.

ACCESS DATA TYPES

Data Type	Description
Short Text (was Text)	The default data type that contains up to 255 characters consisting of any combination of alphabetic and numeric characters—such as names, addresses, and phone numbers—that will not be used to perform calculations.
Long Text (was Memo)	Text entries that contain up to approximately 1 gigabyte (GB) of alphanumeric data. Only the first 64,000 characters display.
Number	Numeric data to be used in mathematical calculations.
Date & Time	Fields that hold date and time values.
Currency	Numeric values representing dollars and cents or fields in which you want to prevent rounding off during calculations.
AutoNumber	Field for which Access assigns a unique, sequential, or random number as records are added to a table. AutoNumber data cannot be modified or deleted.
Yes/No	Single-character entries in a Yes/No format used to enter data that can be only one of two possible values, such as true/false, yes/no, or on/off.
OLE Object	Object, such as a picture, inserted into the database.
Hyperlink	Links to web pages or other files that you access by clicking the links.
Attachment	Any type of file that will be included in the database as an attachment.
Calculated Field	Field created by combining values in other fields within the table.
Lookup Wizard	A field that displays values from another table or from a list of values on the basis of criteria—conditions you set so that you can select the value you want to enter.

Saving Tables   Each object you create in a database must be saved. As you save the database objects, you assign an appropriate name to the object. An appropriate name for each table, then, should help identify the data it holds. After you save the table, Access displays the name you give the table in the Navigation Pane.

HANDS-ON 8.3   Create and Save a Table Using a Datasheet

In this exercise, you will create a table to hold Raritan Clinic East employee data.

1. Double-click the **ID** field column heading to select the text and type **EmployeeNumber**.

2. Press Tab. Then, select **Short Text** from the data type list and type **EmpLastName**.

TIP! In the data type list, notice the underlined mnemonic character. As you enter each column heading and prepare to set the data type, you can use the mnemonic character (such as T for Short Text) to select the data type and then type the field name.

When the fields are not wide enough to display the field name, the field names/column headings truncate because the columns are narrow.

3. Press ⌗Tab⌗ and repeat the procedures outlined in step 2 to enter these short text fields in the order shown:

   a. EmpFirstName

   b. EmpStreet

   c. EmpCity

   d. EmpState

   e. EmpZIP

   f. EmpTelephone

4. Now add these three date fields to the datasheet, ensuring that Date & Time is the data type.

   a. EmpDateHired

   b. EmpTermDate

   c. EmpDOB

In case you can no longer press ⌗Tab⌗ to move to the next field, click the Click to Add field, and then select the data type and change the field name.

 TIP! If any of the data has been misspelled, double-click the field name and retype the field name.

5. Follow these steps to save the table using a new table name:

Ⓐ Click the **Save** button. _____

Ⓑ Type **Raritan Clinic East Employees** in the Table Name field. _____

Ⓒ Click **OK**. _____

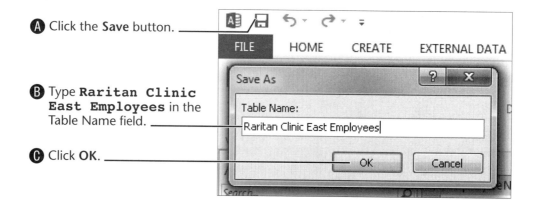

6. Follow these steps to review the table:

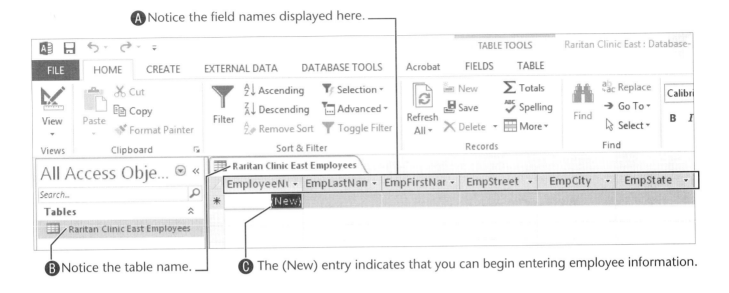

Ⓐ Notice the field names displayed here.

Ⓑ Notice the table name.

Ⓒ The (New) entry indicates that you can begin entering employee information.

Navigating Tables and Entering Data

Now that the table is complete and saved as the first object in the database, you are ready to enter data into the table fields. Because of the column and row layout of the datasheet, moving from field to field within the datasheet is similar to moving among columns and rows of a Word table or cells in an Excel worksheet.

- Press Tab or Enter to move to the next field.

- Press Shift+Tab to move to the previous field.

- Click a field to make it active.

As you access each field, you type the data required for the record. When you complete the data in the last field, pressing Tab or Enter takes you to the first field in the next record. Access saves each record as you complete it, so each new record becomes part of the database table when you move to the next record.

Study the following figure to identify key features of the datasheet as you enter data.

The record/row selector button on the left side of the datasheet enables you to select a record.

As you enter data for a record, a pencil appears in the record/row selector button for the record you are typing.

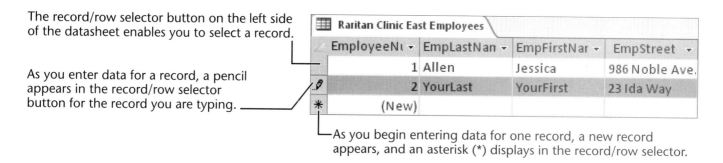

As you begin entering data for one record, a new record appears, and an asterisk (*) displays in the record/row selector.

AutoCorrect

As you may already have discovered when using other Microsoft Office 2013 applications, the AutoCorrect feature helps correct common typographical errors as you enter data just as it does when you mistype common words in Word, Excel, Outlook, or PowerPoint. Data typed into database fields often involves acronyms and proper names, so AutoCorrect functions less frequently.

AutoCorrect is a shared tool in Microsoft Office applications. So, if you have added frequently mistyped words to AutoCorrect while working in Word, Access will automatically correct the same mistyped word. You may also find AutoCorrect a useful tool for expanding acronyms so that they type complex phrases or names. For example, you might enter RCE* into AutoCorrect so that each time you type *RCE* and press Spacebar or Enter, Access and other Office applications will automatically replace *RCE* with *Raritan Clinic East.*

Working with Tabs and Closing Database Objects

As you have learned, when you create a new database, Access starts a blank table and displays it in the work area of the database screen. The tab that appears at the top left of the table displays Table1 until you save the table. Then, the name you assign to the table appears on the tab, in this case, Raritan Clinic East Employees.

As you work with Access and build a database, the number of tables and other objects will grow, so you might have numerous objects open at the same time. When multiple objects are open, Access displays as much of each object as will fit within the work area, and all objects are layered, one on top of the other. The tabs make moving from one object to another more efficient.

At the far right side of the table datasheet window, you will notice the table Close button. To close all open objects at one time, right-click a tab and select Close All.

Each open object in this database is identified by a tab.

The Close button is located at the far right of the tabbed objects.

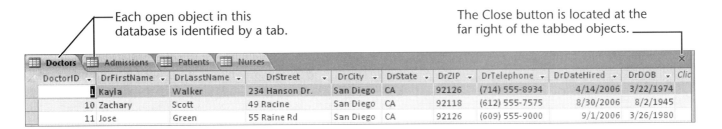

DoctorID ▾	DrFirstName ▾	DrLasstName ▾	DrStreet ▾	DrCity ▾	DrState ▾	DrZIP ▾	DrTelephone ▾	DrDateHired ▾	DrDOB ▾	Clic
1	Kayla	Walker	234 Hanson Dr.	San Diego	CA	92126	(714) 555-8934	4/14/2006	3/22/1974	
10	Zachary	Scott	49 Racine	San Diego	CA	92118	(612) 555-7575	8/30/2006	8/2/1945	
11	Jose	Green	55 Raine Rd	San Diego	CA	92126	(609) 555-9000	9/1/2006	3/26/1980	

HANDS-ON 8.4 Enter Data into a Table Datasheet

In this exercise, you will enter data for two records into the Raritan Clinic East Employees table of the Raritan Clinic East database.

1. Follow these steps to enter data into the first two fields of the first record in the table:

Ⓐ Click the first row of the EmpLastName field.

Ⓑ Type **Allen** and then press Tab.

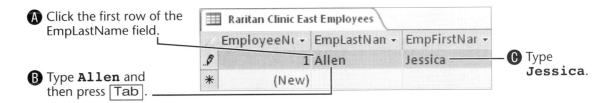

Ⓒ Type **Jessica**.

2. Continue pressing Tab to work through the fields for the record, and enter these values for the first record:

EmpStreet	986 Noble Ave.
EmpCity	San Diego
EmpState	CA
EmpZIP	98109
EmpTelephone	6195553902
EmpDateHired	6/12/2006
EmpDateTerm	
EmpDOB	11/09/1980

3. Press $\boxed{\text{Tab}}$ to create a new record, add your name in the **EmpLastName** and **EmpFirstName** fields, and then complete the second record by entering this data:

EmpStreet	23 Ida Way
EmpCity	San Diego
EmpState	CA
EmpZIP	92126
EmpTelephone	6195551470
EmpDateHired	8/14/2001
EmpDateTerm	
EmpDOB	11/15/1952

4. Press $\boxed{\text{Tab}}$ or $\boxed{\text{Enter}}$ after entering data into the last field to ensure that the record is complete and saved.

Previewing and Printing Data

After entering data into a table datasheet, there may be times when you want to print raw data contained in a table datasheet. Access provides tools for printing all of these objects.

Setting Up Data to Print

When you print from a table datasheet, Access prints the data that actually appears in the datasheet when you issue the print command. You can hide columns to prevent them from printing, change the page layout settings to print the datasheet in landscape layout, and change the margins to fit a datasheet on a single sheet of paper, as you can when you print documents or spreadsheets.

Checking Data Accuracy

Ensuring data accuracy is very important for obtaining meaningful information from the database. In addition, customers and other business contacts are troubled when they see their names misspelled and spot careless data-entry errors. Be sure to check your data for accuracy after it has been entered. One way to do this is to print the contents of your tables. Proofreading a hard copy (paper printout) is often a good way to spot errors.

The Preview Window

Previewing data before printing helps determine adjustments to make to ensure that the datasheet prints on the page as you desire. You can view multiple pages in print preview to see how columns display. You can also see what columns appear on separate pages, and so forth, so you can make the necessary adjustments.

Because the layout of database objects differs, options available in the Print dialog box vary depending on what you are printing. However, the basic procedures used to preview and print database objects are the same and are similar to the procedures used to print files in other applications. When you preview an object, the Print Preview tools appear on the Ribbon. These tools are used to change the layout of the page on which you print.

The Print Preview Ribbon contains tools for changing the layout of the printed document.

Preview settings enable you to change the number of pages displayed onscreen at one time, in this case, part of one page displays at a time.

Close Print Preview restores the Access object window.

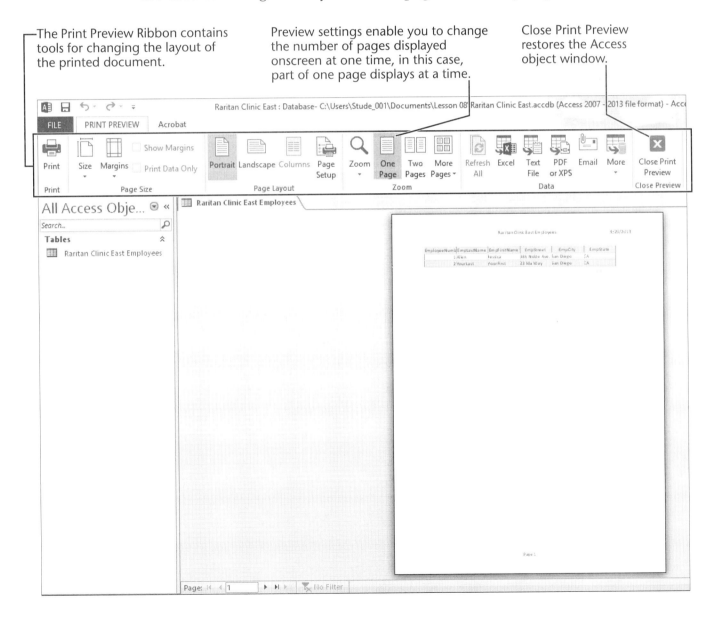

HANDS-ON 8.5 Preview and Print Data

In this exercise, you will preview and print a database table. The Raritan Clinic East Employees table should be open in Access.

1. Choose **File→Print→Print Preview**.

2. Follow these steps to preview the datasheet:

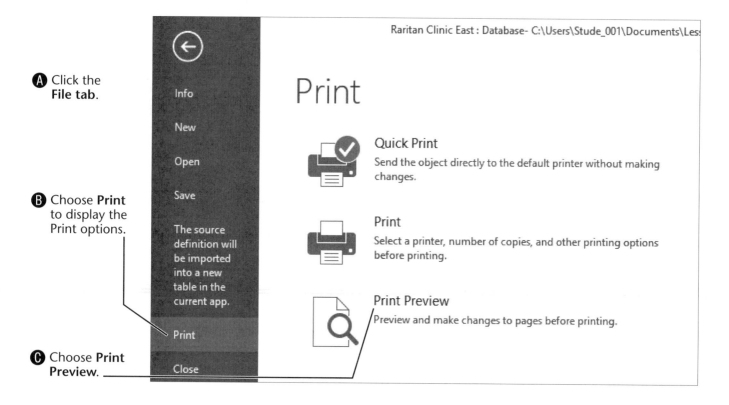

A Click the **File tab**.

B Choose **Print** to display the Print options.

C Choose **Print Preview**.

Raritan Clinic East : Database- C:\Users\Stude_001\Documents\Les

Print

Quick Print
Send the object directly to the default printer without making changes.

Print
Select a printer, number of copies, and other printing options before printing.

Print Preview
Preview and make changes to pages before printing.

3. Follow these steps to view pages that will print:

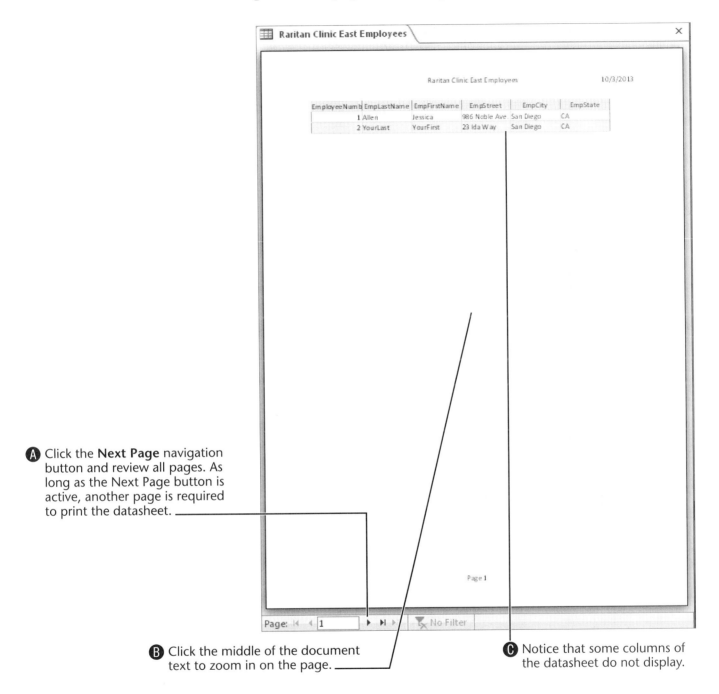

Raritan Clinic East Employees

Raritan Clinic East Employees   10/3/2013

EmployeeNumb	EmpLastName	EmpFirstName	EmpStreet	EmpCity	EmpState
1	Allen	Jessica	986 Noble Ave.	San Diego	CA
2	YourLast	YourFirst	23 Ida Way	San Diego	CA

Page 1

Page: ◄ ◄ 1 ► ►►   ⧩ No Filter

A Click the **Next Page** navigation button and review all pages. As long as the Next Page button is active, another page is required to print the datasheet.

B Click the middle of the document text to zoom in on the page.

C Notice that some columns of the datasheet do not display.

4. Follow these steps to display multiple pages in the preview window:

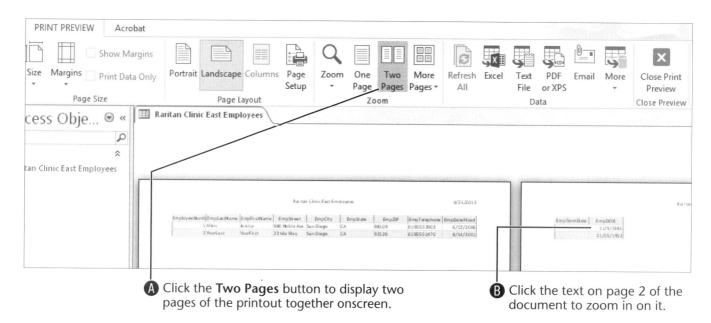

A Click the **Two Pages** button to display two pages of the printout together onscreen.

B Click the text on page 2 of the document to zoom in on it.

5. Choose **Print Preview→Page Layout→Landscape** to display more of the datasheet on one page.

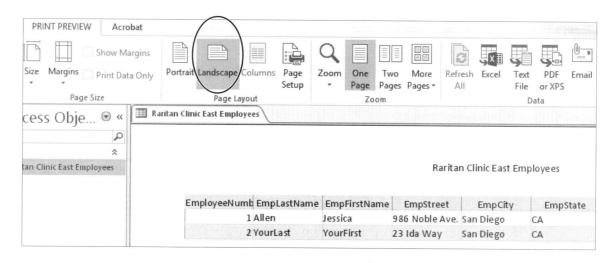

Landscape layout makes the page wider to display more columns on a page.

6. Choose **Print Preview**→**Print**→**Print** to open the Print dialog box.

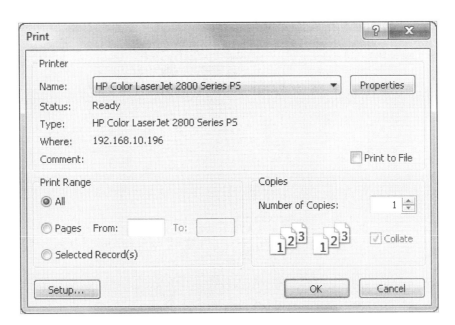

The Print dialog box you see may be different from the one shown here based on your active printer.

7. Select **Selected Record(s)** in the Print dialog box to print the current record, or **page 1** of the datasheet.

8. Click **OK** to print. Otherwise, click **Cancel**.

9. **Close** ⊠ the table. Choose **No** when prompted to save changes.

10. If necessary, close the Navigation Pane.

Closing a Database and Exiting Access

After all objects in a database are closed, you can close the database and exit Access. The procedures used to perform these tasks are the same as those used to close files and exit other Office applications. Use these techniques to close a database and exit Access:

- Choose the File tab and select Close to close the database.

- Press Alt+F4 from the keyboard to exit Access.

- Click the Access 2013 application window Close ⊠ button.

Because Access databases contain numerous objects, it's always a good idea to close each database properly before exiting Access. This ensures that all objects in the database are saved and closed carefully.

HANDS-ON 8.6 Close a Database and Exit Access

In this exercise, you will close the Raritan Clinic East database and exit Access.

1. Choose **File→Close**.

2. Click the Access 2013 application window **Close** ☒ button.

# Concepts Review

To check your knowledge of the key concepts introduced in this lesson, complete the Concepts Review quiz here. Or, take the quiz online by going to the student resource center.

True/False Questions

			Page number
1. Access databases may contain multiple types of objects.	**true**	**false**	_____
2. Access databases can hold only one of each object type.	**true**	**false**	_____
3. The basic unit of data in a database is referred to as a field.	**true**	**false**	_____
4. Every table should have a primary key field.	**true**	**false**	_____
5. All data about one item is referred to as a file.	**true**	**false**	_____
6. A primary key field holds duplicate data.	**true**	**false**	_____

Multiple Choice Questions

7. Which Access database object holds the data in a database?

Page number: _____

a. Forms

b. Queries

c. Reports

d. Tables

8. Which statement about the relationship between fields and records and files is true?

Page number: _____

a. A record is made up of multiple fields.

b. A field is made up of multiple records.

c. A field is made up of multiple files.

d. All of the above

9. What purpose does a database table serve?

Page number: _____

a. As the basic object used to store data

b. As a backup copy of database data

c. As a database window

d. None of the above

10. Which of the following represents the structural relationship among data elements from smallest to largest?

Page number: _____

a. File, Field, Record

b. Record, File, Field

c. Field, Record, File

d. Record, Field, File

Skill Builders

SKILL BUILDER 8.1 Create a New Database with a Table

First Perk is a coffee shop that is getting ready to open in your town. Before opening, they would like to have a database in place that will enable them to track sales, supplies, menu items, etc. In this exercise, you will create the First Perk database and the first table.

1. Launch **Access** and click the **Blank desktop database** icon.

2. Type **sb-First Perk** in the File Name text box and click the **Browse** folder to select a folder in which to save the database. Click **OK**.

3. Choose **Create** to create the database.

4. Change the ID field name to **ItemNumber** and then enter these field names into the **Table1** column headings, selecting the data type shown for each field:

Field Name	Data Type
ItemName	Short Text
Price	Currency

5. Save the table using the table name **Menu Items**.

6. Add the following records to the **Menu Items** table:

Item Name	Price
Cappuccino	2
Latte	3

7. If directed by your instructor, print a copy of the datasheet.

8. Close the database.

SKILL BUILDER 8.2 **Create a Database Using a Template**

In this exercise, you will create a new database using the Tasks template.

1. Launch **Access**, if it is closed, and choose **File→New**.

   Access displays a list of sample databases in the Backstage view.

2. Follow these steps to select the database type and save the new database:

Ⓐ Click in the search bar that displays *Search for online templates*, type **tasks**, and press Enter.

Ⓑ In the **Category** list, select **Task List**.

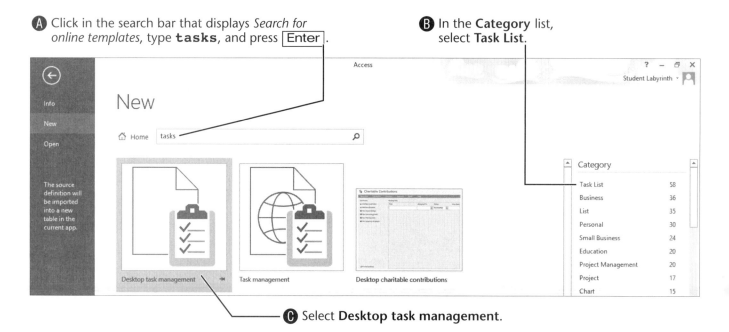

Ⓒ Select **Desktop task management**.

3. Type the name **sb-Semester Tasks**, navigate to your file storage location, and click **OK**. Then click **Create**.

   ⚠️**TIP!** If the Getting Started dialog box displays, just close it.

   Access downloads the template, saves it using the filename you assigned, and opens the database.

Review Database Objects

4. Enable content, if necessary, open the Navigation Pane, and then change the display in the Navigation Pane to display objects by **Object Type**.

5. Open each table, form, query, and report and review the arrangement of data in each object.

6. Close the database.

Glossary

AutoComplete Feature that recognizes certain kinds of entries, such as dates, and offers to complete them for you as you type

AutoCorrect Feature that automatically corrects commonly misspelled words as you type, based on a built-in dictionary

Backstage View Feature that contains commands to manage your files, such as Open, Save, and Print; available from the File tab

Cell Small rectangle that appears wherever a column and row intersect in a table or spreadsheet

Character Formatting How text or numerical characters look; includes font type, font style, font size, font color, and special effects

Clip Art Collection of photos, images, and pictures you can use in your documents

Clipboard Area in your computer's memory where data that you cut or copy is temporarily stored before pasting it in another location

Compatibility Mode Documents created in earlier versions of Microsoft Office open in Compatibility Mode; this limits the application to using only features available in earlier versions

Contextual Tabs Tabs on the Ribbon that appear only when certain objects are selected; for example, the Table Tools→Layout contextual tab appears only when a table is selected in Word or PowerPoint

Crop Feature used to hide any unwanted portions of a graphic image

Data Type Category of data that determines the type of data a field can contain, such as numeric, alphanumeric, date, or currency

Database Collection of related information (e.g., name and address list); typically stored in an electronic format that allows users to select and sort records of information

Field Column of information in a database

File Collection of data saved on your hard drive or other storage media; saved documents are called files

File Format Consistent pattern for storing information in a computer file; application programs normally have a special file format that they use by default; examples are docx (Word), xlsx (Excel), pptx (PowerPoint), and accdb (Access)

Find and Replace Feature that finds a word, phrase, or format that you specify and, optionally, replaces it with another word, phrase, or format

Folder Area in a computer filing system in which you store files (documents); can be made on storage devices, such as USB drives, hard drives, or network drives

Formula Equation that performs calculations on values in a spreadsheet

Formula Bar Data in the active cell appears in the Formula Bar

Freeze Panes   Excel feature that allows you to freeze column or row headings so they remain visible on the screen when you scroll through a spreadsheet

Function   Formula built into Excel that performs calculations on cells in a table or spreadsheet

Handles   Small squares or circles that surround an object when it is selected; you can drag a handle with the mouse pointer to resize an object

I-beam   Shape of the mouse pointer when in the typing area of a document; resembles a capital "I"

Icon   Small GUI (graphical user interface) that represents an object, such as a folder in which you store your files

Insertion Point   Blinking indicator where text will appear on the screen; when typing you must position the insertion point at the desired location before typing; also referred to as the cursor

Live Preview   When pointing at formatting commands on the Ribbon, Live Preview displays how the format would appear on selected text and objects without actually applying the format

Mathematical Operators   Signs used for addition, subtraction, multiplication, and division

Mini Toolbar   Contains frequently used formatting commands; appears when you select cells or text or when you right-click on cells or text

Name Box   Displays the address of the active cell

Nonprinting Characters   Symbols that represent typing elements, such as spaces and tabs; you can display the symbols on the screen, but they will not appear on the printed page

Presentation Program   Software application (such as PowerPoint) that allows you to create dynamic multimedia presentations that can be displayed on your computer or projected on a screen

Primary Key   Unique identifier in a database field (e.g., a social security number); helps ensure that a database does not contain duplicate records

Quick Access Toolbar   Toolbar that contains buttons for frequently used commands; can be customized by adding command buttons

Range   Group of adjacent cells in a spreadsheet, such as A1:A100

Record   Row of information in a database

Redo   Feature that allows you to successively repeat your last action(s), starting with the most recent

Relative Reference   Excel automatically changes cell addresses in copied formulas and functions relative to where they are copied

Ribbon   Band running across the top of the screen that contains software commands for Office 2013 applications; organized in tabs that relate to a particular type of activity and groups that contain related commands

Scroll Bar   Means of moving to different areas of a document

Select   To choose an object or to highlight text in order to manipulate it in some way

Selection Bar   In Word, the white space at the left margin from which you can select text

Slide Layout   Preset layout of placeholder boxes on a PowerPoint slide

Slide Show   View used in PowerPoint when delivering a presentation

Sort   Arranges data in alphabetic, numeric, or date order

Spelling Checker   Feature that monitors your spelling as you type; underlines suspected misspellings with wavy red lines; right-clicking displays a pop-up menu of possible correct spellings

Spreadsheet   Document that allow you to organize data in columns and rows, analyze data, and perform calculations on data; also known as worksheet

Suite   Collection of software applications sold as one package; less expensive than buying the individual applications; applications typically contain features that work in a similar fashion

Task Pane   Screen element that contains links and icons you click to issue commands to the computer

Template   Serves as a pattern for new documents, which take on the template's characteristics, such as font choice, line spacing, margin settings, boilerplate text, etc.

Theme   Set of formatting selections you can apply to a document; includes colors, graphic elements, and fonts all designed to work well together

Toolbar   GUI (graphical user interface) containing buttons that represent commands

ToolTips   Small pop-up notes that appear when you hover the mouse pointer over a Ribbon or toolbar command; contain a description of the command

Typing Area   In Word, the area between the margins of a page; where you type

Undo   Feature that successively undoes changes you make in a document, starting with the last one

USB Flash Drive   Stores your data on a flash memory chip; plug it into a USB port on any computer and Windows recognizes it as an additional disk drive

Views   Varying ways you can look at a document, spreadsheet, or presentation; optimized for specific types of work

Word Processor   Software application that allows you to electronically create and edit text

Word Wrap   Feature that wraps to the next line a long string of text that extends beyond the right margin

Worksheet   *See* Spreadsheet

WordArt   Graphic image of stylized, decorative text

Index

Compatibility Mode, 10
Compatibility Pack, 36
contextual tabs, 7
Convert command, 11
copying
    cell data, 129–130
    formulas and functions, 153–155
    text, 67–69
cover letter, 27–34
cropping images, 99–101
Currency data type, 225
custom web apps, 217
cut/copy and paste functions, 67–69

D
data, defined, 215
data accuracy, 230
databases
    closing database, 235–236
    closing objects, 228–229
    creating from blank, 218–219
    data types, 224–225
    defined, 215, 222
    designing, 218, 224
    entering data, 227–228, 229–230
    navigating in, 220–221
    previewing data, 230–235
    printing data, 230–235
    saving, 225–227
    tables in, 221–230
    template-based, 217
Datasheet View, 222–223
data types, database fields, 224–225, 226
Date & Time data type, 225
documents
    (*see also* text)
    bulleted lists, 33–34
    closing, 15–16
    creating new, 16–17
    navigating in, 12–15
    opening, 10–11
    printing, 39–40
    saving, 34–38
    selecting entire, 60
    tables in, 40–43, 47
    versions of Word, 10–11
DOCX and DOC file formats, 36

E
editing tools, 62–67
embedded charts, 158–163
Enter button in Excel, 122–123
Enter key in Word, 31–32
envelopes, 48–49
equals sign in formulas, 146
Excel
    (*see also* charts; formulas; spreadsheets)
    defined, 111
    entering data, 122–126
    mouse pointer shapes, 116
    navigating in, 112, 114
    overview, 3
    starting, 111, 113
    window elements, 112

F
fields, database, 221, 222, 223–224
file, database object, 222
file formats, 36
File tab, 6, 114, 184
Find and Replace dialog box, 71
finding
    clip art, 95, 195–196
    text, 70–73
folders
    definition, 88
    naming, 89
fonts, 83–88, 194
foreign key fields, 224
formatting
    borders, 47
    bulleted lists, 33–34
    cells, 41–43
    charts, 165
    field data, 224
    fonts, 83–88
    nonprinting characters, 29
    paragraphs, 27–29, 30–31, 90
    presentation slides, 194
    tables, 47
    text characters, 27–29, 30–31, 83–88, 194
    WordArt, 91–95
Formula Bar, 114